A **Golf Digest** B O O K

Leadbetter's
Quick Tips

The Very Best Short Lessons to
Fix Any Part of Your Game

By David Leadbetter
with Scott Smith

Doubleday
New York   London   Toronto   Sydney   Auckland

PUBLISHED BY DOUBLEDAY

Golf Digest is a registered trademark of Condé Nast Publications.
Copyright © 2006 Golf Digest Publications.

All Rights Reserved

Published in the United States by Doubleday, an imprint of
The Doubleday Broadway Publishing Group,
a division of Random House, Inc., New York.
www.doubleday.com

DOUBLEDAY and the portrayal of an anchor with a dolphin are
registered trademarks of Random House, Inc.

*Photography by Stephen Szurlej, Dom Furore, J.D. Cuban, Darren Carroll,
Gary Newkirk, Rusty Jarrett, Ben Van Hook, PGA Tour.*

Illustrations by Paul Lipp

Book design by Edward Mann

Cataloging-in-Publication Data is on file with the Library of Congress.

ISBN-13: 978-0-385-51193-3
ISBN-10: 0-385-51193-0

PRINTED IN THE UNITED STATES OF AMERICA

10 9 8 7 6 5 4 3 2 1

First Edition

CONTENTS

INTRODUCTION

I've always believed in an approach to instruction that focuses on the fundamentals. I'm not interested in giving a golfer a quick tip that doesn't last; my goal as a teacher is to help golfers develop a repeatable swing that allows them to strike the ball with authority and control. Out on the practice tee, this means giving my students an understanding of where they are, showing them where to get to and then giving them a road map to help them get there. "There" means owning a flowing, rhythmic swing that's built on the fundamentals shared by all good players yet is uniquely yours.

But I realize that in today's fast-paced society, most people don't have time to practice as much as they used to. Most golfers just want to go out and play. And they want to have something that works—a drill, an image or a sensation—that they can put into use quickly out on the golf course.

In this day and age, with so much technology at our disposal, it would be easy to make learning the golf swing very complex. At our worldwide headquarters at ChampionsGate in Orlando, we help players of every level improve by utilizing high-speed video, tracking on-course stats, analyzing biomechanics, and even assessing their level of fitness. But as great as all this high-tech information is in identifying a player's specific problems and faults, the "fix" still must be communicated in a simple, easy-to-understand manner.

Most tour players don't want to hear a million things about the swing. They want us to cut to the chase, they want to know cause and effect, they want to be able to communicate in such a way that they can use the information in a fairly short space of time.

That's the theory behind my teaching, and the philosophy behind this collection of tips—assembled from the instruction articles I've written for Golf Digest over the past 10 years.

Think of these quick tips not as band-aids but as bricks, bricks you're laying one at a time, tip by tip, to build a fundamentally solid swing. Use these tips as benchmarks to improve in a way and at a pace that's right for you.

Though all these tips are built on solid fundamentals, there's still an element of trial and error involved. A tip can be right for one person and wrong for another. That's the beauty of a quick tip: You can go out and say, "I tried that, but it didn't work, but this other one worked great . . ."

I've come to realize that you have to be versatile in giving a golfer swing advice. What I say might hit home to one person but not another. You've got to hit on the right cue, which sends the right message. Like a row of bricks, there's a continuity to these tips, taking you from setup to finish, from tee to green. Some may seem repetitive, but that's because they're saying the same things in a different way. A good teacher communicates in a way that benefits each student.

With some tour players what we talk about might be partly technical, or it might be simple and feel-oriented. Funny, but what I've found working with a lot of amateurs is that they frequently seem to want *more* technical information than many of the pros.

Too many golfers stand over the ball with intense mechanical swing thoughts that just create tension, and too much tension prevents a golfer from developing a flowing, rhythmic swing motion. Understanding the fundamentals is important, but creating good motion is really what it's all about.

That's why I'm a big believer in teaching by images. They help you generate good mechanics without overthinking. At its best, a swing image is memorable without being too specific. I've found that by staying general—*stretch your backswing like an archer pulls a bowstring*—it's then up to the player to interpret the golf move that goes with that image.

Some golfers prefer to get their information via drills or specific movements. A good example is Charles Howell III, who likes to have something technical to work on. If you're this type of player, you'll find this book chockful of easy-to-use drills covering every aspect of the swing.

Other golfers learn best by example, by modeling their swing movements after a particular player they admire or feel a similarity with in terms of body size and shape or even temperament.

Whether it's based on a drill, an image or tour role model, if a tip allows you to get to a root cause of a swing problem, it can act as a catalyst. By changing one thing, you, in turn, can change another thing.

After all, how does any golfer build a solid swing? Brick by brick, tip by tip.

David Leadbetter
ChampionsGate
February 2006

ACKNOWLEDGMENTS

Having enjoyed a longstanding relationship with Golf Digest, I feel this book is a true reflection of the quality work that the magazine and its staff consistently delivers to their readers. To Scott Smith, Golf Digest's Director of Instruction over these past few years, thank you for your inspiration and for reminding me that we had enough "quick tips" to write a book—literally!

Special thanks also to instruction writers and editors Ron Kaspriske, Matt Rudy and Peter Morrice for making the content fit and flow so well. My thanks also goes to Golf Digest photographers J.D. Cuban, Dom Furore and Stephen Szurlej for their outstanding work with the camera. Finally, thanks to Paul Lipp for his memorable illustrations, and to Design Director Ed Mann for his vision and enthusiasm.

D.L.

CHAPTER ONE

Getting Started:
Pre-Swing
Fundamentals

Improving your fundamentals—which starts with how you set up and address the ball—can go a long way toward improving your dynamics (how you actually hit the ball). ● It's absolutely necessary to develop an athletic "ready" position at address to make a good, repeatable swing that allows you to strike the ball solidly. ● Here are my best quick tips to help you set up properly, develop a grip that's right for your game, get aligned accurately and focus precisely on your target.

Getting Started: Pre-Swing Fundamentals

Every good golf shot begins with a solid foundation

The proper setup in golf is all-important. It forms the foundation for a consistent, repetitive swing. If your grip is faulty, or your address position is flawed, you'll have to perform compensations to hit the ball solidly.

I was not a big fan of geometry in school, but in teaching the game of golf, I've come to realize the importance of it. Whether the subject is body angles or shaft plane or clubface angle, being aware of the geometry of the swing is a big factor in learning to play consistent golf.

The greatest awareness of golf's geometry should be at address: That's when you are getting the clubface square, or perpendicu-lar, to the target and creating the proper angles formed by the forward-leaning upper body in relation to the shaft, hanging arms and lower body.

Adopting a good posture is what it's all about. Observe Retief Goosen just after impact *(left)*. The angle formed by the right side of his body is almost a replica of the position he was in at address. His body is more open to the target than it was initially, but by retaining the original angle, it's hard for him to hit too many wild shots. And improving the quality of your bad shots is the key to scoring your best, whether you're a world-class pro or weekend golfer.

Retief Goosen's solid ball-striking is the result of retaining the body angles established at address.

Create the proper angles
How to position your body and arms at address

To get yourself in a good posture at address, try this simple drill: Set your 5-iron in front of you, as I'm doing in the first photo on the right. Now lean on the club by bending from the hip sockets to get into what I call a "ready" position, **the knees slightly flexed and the upper back straight, not rounded**. You want to feel as if you're engaging your abdominal muscles.

As you place the clubhead behind the ball *(second photo, right)*, your elbows should be pointing toward their corresponding hip joints. Turn them slightly in and rotate your forearms in and up, much as a setter in volleyball would prepare to "bump" the ball.

You should feel some pressure under your armpits, between your upper arms and chest. If you cannot feel this, your arms are out of position.

Stay relaxed, your arms hanging freely to form a triangle. Start your swing with the triangle moving in sync with the turning of your body. You'll then have a much better chance to set off a chain reaction of good positions and smooth motion throughout the swing.

Rotate your forearms in and up, much as a setter in volleyball would to "bump" the ball.

Sit up for a better setup
Hold your stomach firm

For a solid set-up position, firm up your stomach at address. Feel the same stabilizing tension in your abdominal muscles as you do when you perform a sit-up.

This image helps you keep your lower back straight and your pelvis tilted properly, though **your shoulders and neck muscles remain relaxed**. You can now maintain the body angles set at address throughout the swing, which is the key to a better impact position and more consistent shotmaking.

Bend from the hip sockets, the knees slightly flexed and the upper back straight, not rounded. Feel as if you're engaging your abdominal muscles.

PAUL LIFF

Spring into action
For an athletic setup, think 'play ball'

Like a baseball player poised to field a ground-ball—or to swing for the fences— the good golfer at address appears **relaxed, balanced and ready to spring into action.**

There are many similarities in the dynamics of baseball and golf, which is apparent in the photos below of baseball great (and scratch golfer) Mark McGwire. There should be a sense of liveliness in your feet and legs. The stance is wide enough to promote stability yet narrow enough to allow for a proper weight shift and free-flowing turning motion with the lower body.

Flex your knees so your kneecaps are directly over the balls of your feet. Stick your rear end out a bit while keeping your lower back fairly straight. From this springy, athletic position you're now ready to "play ball."

A sound setup is essential to every athletic swing, whether you're swinging for the fences or the fairways.

Make a fluid start
How to begin with good rhythm

For a smooth start to your swing, imagine you're holding a bucket full of water that you want to swing backward without spilling a drop. If you jerk the bucket back in the manner many golfers snatch the club away, you'd spill plenty.

That's why I encourage golfers to develop some sort of trigger to start the swing. The trigger can be a subtle inward movement of the right knee or a slight forward press of the hands. Picture the water bucket—**it's easier to swing it back smoothly if you start with a slight rocking motion forward.**

Everything is geared to a smooth takeaway. If you begin with good rhythm, you'll maintain good rhythm throughout the swing.

Everything is geared to a smooth take-away. If you begin with good rhythm, you'll maintain good rhythm throughout the swing.

Groove a good grip
Both hands work as a unit

In the golf swing, **the hands should remain passive,** serving primarily to link the club with the body. Too often, golfers allow one hand to dominate the other during the swing.

To get your hands working together, think of the left thumb fitting into the right palm, just as two pieces of wood are joined in tongue-and-groove fashion.

First, take hold of the club with the left hand so the left thumb rests on the top of the grip. Next, place your right hand on the underside of the grip, with the shaft crossing diagonally from the base of the little finger to the first joint of the index finger. Complete the grip by fitting the left thumb (tongue) into the hollow of the right palm, underneath the thumb pad (groove).

Your hands can now work together as a unit to transfer the power generated by the motion of the swing squarely to the back of the ball.

Make it a snug fit to prevent any regripping of the club at the top or one hand dominating the other at impact.

Place the palms 'parallel'
Why a neutral grip is the best option

A neutral grip requires no compensations later in the swing and less manipulation of the clubhead through impact. A neutral grip is one in which the "V" formed by your left thumb and index finger points to your right eye. A grip is "strong" when both hands are turned more to the right; it's "weak" when the hands are more toward the left.

The key to any good grip is that **your hands are parallel to one another**. Check this by holding the club up in front of you at eye level. The creases formed by each thumb and index finger should be parallel. Another way to check: When you place the club behind the ball, check the angles formed at the back of each wrist: They should be virtually symmetrical.

If you tend to slice, turn the lines a bit to your right, adopting a stronger grip. If you hook, turn them a bit to your left.

When working on your grip, it's easier to assume the correct position of your hands if you hold the club out in front of you.

Square your shoulders
Get parallel to the target line

Most golfers assume that if their toes are lined up parallel to the target line, their alignment is correct.

Wrong. **Your shoulders play a vital role in proper alignment.** To ensure that your shoulders are neither open nor closed in relation to your target, hold the head of the club in your right hand and lay the shaft across your chest and left shoulder. Make sure the butt end of the club points parallel to your target line, not to the left as is the case with most slicers, or to the right, as it does with most hookers.

Get your shots headed in the right direction by making sure your shoulders, not just your toes, are parallel to the target line.

Trade tension for rhythm
Why you should whistle while you swing

Too often golfers lack rhythm in their swings because they are too tense at address. Much of this tension can be attributed to golfers holding their breath.

When you exhale properly during the swing, your muscles become more relaxed. That's why I often tell golfers to whistle softly while they swing. As you step up to the ball, breathe through your nose, then exhale and whistle as you start the club back. Do this all the way through the finish of your swing.

Practice this breathing routine the next time you hit balls, and you will find that **timing your breathing with the swing will reduce tension and improve rhythm,** resulting in a better shot.

You see it all the time: A golfer at address, mouth set in a rigid grimace. He's already lost his best chance to make a powerful, rhythmic swing.

Develop a pre-shot routine

Prepare to hit the shot the same way each time

One of the defining attributes of tour pros is that each one has a consistent pre-shot routine. The routine not only helps a player get comfortable and in rhythm, but it also is necessary for proper ball position and accurate alignment.

Routines vary from player to player. Develop one of your own liking that you think will become natural and automatic. Then **follow it with each shot.** This will be a significant step in achieving consistency in your game. Watching the pros on television can help you develop a solid pre-shot routine.

How Fred Funk sets up to a shot never varies—a key to his driving accuracy.

Zero in on your target
For greater accuracy, magnify your view

After you've assessed the shot at hand and selected the proper club, take a last, "absorbing" look at your target, as though you were seeing it through a magnifying glass.

This allows you to **filter out distractions** as you visualize how you want the ball to fly, land and finish.

Focusing on a specific target gives you a sense that—whether it's the flag on a par 3 or a tree trunk beyond the fairway on a longer hole—you have less room for error, and your body will respond with a more precise swing.

An essential step in any good pre-shot routine is selecting the smallest, most specific target possible.

CHAPTER TWO

Off the Tee:
Longer &
Straighter Drives

The goal of any golfer is to develop a repeatable swing that allows you to strike the ball with authority and control. It means owning a swing that's built on fundamentals, yet is uniquely yours, and having confidence in that swing so that you can maximize power, especially off the tee. In this chapter I'm going to identify and describe my tee-shot fundamentals, give examples of how the best golfers put them to use, and show you ways to incorporate them into your game.

Driving with more power and accuracy

For longer, straighter tee shots, focus on the fundamentals

There might be surer ways to lower your scores—knocking approach shots close to the hole and sinking more putts, to name two—but let's face it: Who doesn't want to really nail your drives long and straight? And do it shot after shot.

Now that we've got you gripping the club better and setting up to the ball properly, let's work on making powerful contact with the driver.

First, the good news for the average golfer: To hit the ball far and straight doesn't require you to be a bulked-up jock—far from it. **To strike a golf ball solidly and consistently on line requires the proper timing of** **the swing's two main components—the rotating body and the swinging arms, hands and club.**

Shown here launching a 300-yard drive, Charles Howell III is proof of that. He's not a big man—though deceptively strong at 160 pounds—but he's one of the long drivers on tour. His source of power? He has tremendous coil and leverage, great balance and timing.

That's the goal of any golf swing: to get all of these parts moving in the proper sequence, a chain reaction that results in the clubhead being delivered powerfully and squarely onto the ball. In this chapter, I'll show you how.

Charles Howell's power isn't due to sheer strength—it stems from great balance, coil, leverage and timing.

Hit up on the ball
To launch your drives, practice on an upslope

Many golfers set up with the driver the way they do with an iron and then hit down on the ball. Instead, learn **to sweep the ball off the tee** by practicing the correct set-up position on an upslope. Place more weight on your right side, with the left hip bumped slightly forward and your spine tilted slightly to the right. Now take this launch position to the tee.

This is one of Vijay Singh's favorite drills. Hit balls off an upslope on the range; remember to finish with your weight forward.

Get maximum carry and roll
How to optimize your launch angle and spin rate

It's important for players to get the right image of what they're trying to do at impact. For wood shots—the driver especially—**you want a slightly ascending, sweeping blow with no contact with the turf.** This will give you maximum carry and roll, and less sidespin.

Think of how you kick a soccer ball: Your foot glides just above the ground and then rises upward to hit the ball just below its equator. That's the same basic angle of approach you want to create with your driver.

Using a new, big-headed driver? Tee the ball high, with at least half of the ball above the top of the clubface.

Swing with better rhythm
Take a tip from an elephant

There's a steady, rhythmic flow to every good golf swing. It begins with the turning of the chest to initiate a smooth, slow takeaway.

As you start your backswing, imagine that your arms are as loose and limber as an elephant's trunk. Just as an elephant moves its trunk by first moving its head, so should your upper torso initiate the backward motion of the arms and club.

This image is also an effective one for the transition. The motion of the downswing begins with a move of the body back toward the target as the club is still reaching the top. Therefore, the club and the body will briefly be going in opposite directions—just as an elephant's trunk lags behind the head as it swings down.

There should be very little tension in the arms on the takeaway; your chest starts the backward motion of the swing.

Start back in sync
How to move your arms and body in unison

Michelle Wie is a phenom that comes along only once every era. It would be impossible for her to keep improving at the rate she has in the past few years, so her goal is to improve steadily, in smaller increments. That's a lesson for all golfers.

Restrict your practice sessions to one specific move. Case in point: In the photo above, taken at the 2005 Sony Open, we're working on getting Michelle's arms to swing back in sync with her body on the most efficient path off the ball, with the proper amount of forearm rotation. Distilled into a single swing thought: **Push away from the target with the left arm and shoulder.** Work on that move until it produces a smooth blending of the arms and torso on the backswing.

If you can get your takeaway right, then your timing is likely to be good. This is especially important with the driver.

Make a big turn . . .
Save the coil for last

PERFECT

NO

Here I've turned my torso too early. Now I'll have to lift the club to the top without a power-producing coiling motion.

If you think of the body turn only in terms of "how much," it's probably going to happen out of sequence. **The key concern is "how and when."**

To make that big turn, many golfers turn their hips and right shoulder too early. When you max out the turning of the body by the time the arms are only halfway back, not only do you drag the club too far inside (*small photo, left*), but the tendency is then to lift the arms up in a weak motion to complete the backswing.

The drill I'm demonstrating on the right will help you incorporate this "all together now" movement into your backswing.

... At the right time
Keep the arms in front of the turning chest

Ideally, the arms and the body complete the turn at the same time, with the real coiling happening in the last third of the backswing. It's that final stretch at the top that gives a good backswing its dynamic look.

To maximize your windup, feel as if your body completes the backswing, not your arms. The drill here will prevent an early turn and help synchronize your arm swing and body turn.

Swing the club under your right arm to keep the right side in place, then complete the backswing with the arms and body turning in sync. The key is to **keep the arms and clubhead in front of the turning body as you swing back.**

STEP 1

STEP 2

To maximize your windup, feel as if your body completes the backswing, not your arms.

How to check your plane
Stay inside 'the Golden Triangle'

Though important for consistency, the swing plane can be difficult to visualize. But you don't need to stress out about it.

Simply put, you're on an OK plane halfway back when your hands are opposite your chest and **the butt of the club points somewhere within what I call "the Golden Triangle"** (*photo, left*). Use a mirror to check your positions. Getting the club in this general plane location going back improves your chances of being on the correct plane in the all-important downswing.

As you finish coiling back from here to the top of the swing, be sure to keep the axis of your spine consistent. Don't lift or dip.

Swing against a wall
How to keep on plane to the top

Many players have trouble sensing what a correct, on-plane position feels like as they near the top of the swing. Here's an effective image to use, with or without a club.

Imagine your backside is against a wall. Make your normal backswing; if your hands were to smack into the wall, your swing plane is too flat. If your hands seem to be radically moving away from the wall as you get to the top, your plane is too steep.

The key is to **make sure your hands swing up on the "slot" between your back and the wall.** Use this imaginary wall—or a real one—to check your plane, then incorporate that feeling into your swing.

Get on the right plane at the top, and you won't have to make compensations on the downswing.

Improve your lower-body action
Keep the right knee flexed

Good leg action is vital for a balanced, dynamic swing. But overuse of the legs at the wrong moment can undermine the real power source: the hips.

For high-handicappers, the problem typically is too much leg movement at the start of the backswing. Low-handicappers often overuse their legs starting the downswing.

Look at the swings of great players and you'll find **virtually all of the leg action occurs through impact.**

Know when to "get legs." Begin with a dynamic position at address: feet evenly angled out, knees slightly flexed and weight balanced on the balls of your feet.

You want a feeling in your legs of resistance going back, softness starting down, acceleration through impact and balance at the finish.

Nick Faldo winds his upper torso over a stable, yet flexed right knee—the key to creating and storing power on the backswing.

Brace yourself on the way back
Create more leverage

The left-foot-back drill is an excellent way to feel the building of resistance with the lower body. As you set up to the ball, pull your left foot back so the toe is in line with your right heel, as I'm demonstrating at right. Now lift your left heel slightly off the ground. As you swing back, **feel as though you're "sitting" into a braced right knee.** You'll feel resistance created in your right thigh as you wind up the bigger muscles in the hips and upper torso.

After several practice swings using this drill, return to your normal set-up position and focus on maintaining the resistance in the right side all the way to the top of the swing.

During the backswing, the primary role of the legs is to resist the coiling of the upper body. It's how you develop leverage in the swing.

27

Set your swing for more power

To complete your backswing, 'pull the arrow' all the way back

Want more snap on your downswing? Think of what happens when an archer draws a bowstring back: The more the archer pulls the bowstring taut, the farther the arrow will fly.

This stretch-and-release image is ideal for golfers. **The more stretch and width you create on your backswing, the more energy you're able to store.** You've created maximum torque and established maximum width. You then release the energy by uncoiling the torso on the downswing and letting the club rip through the impact area.

Obviously, it's important to maintain your flexibility, particularly as you get older—otherwise you won't be able to pull the bowstring back very far.

Stretch your backswing just as an archer pulls a bowstring taut.

How to develop and retain torque
Turn the upper body as the lower body resists

The coiling and uncoiling of the torso, with resistance and stability in the lower body, is required to provide leverage. This motion initiates an energy transfer that produces natural speed to the arms and hands. **The lower body leads the way, followed by the upper body, arms, hands and club.** To sustain this leverage the left leg must straighten through impact.

Practice this sequential motion with a club behind your back (*left*). Move into your top-of-swing position, then continue into the downswing, turning the upper body through as the lower body resists. Keep your spine angle the same as you established at address. This drill helps you focus on the role your abdominal muscles play in creating and retaining torque.

The coiling of the upper torso over a stable and resisting lower body is the most powerful move in the swing.

For more consistency, get into 'the slot'
How to make a picture-perfect transition

Davis Love III's top-of-swing position that you see above is fundamentally solid and almost guarantees a great shot. Here's what you can learn from it:

• Note the full turn and windup with the upper body, **left shoulder under chin, back facing target**.

• The left knee is behind the ball, and the weight is fully on the right side.

• The right elbow supports the club, with the hands high.

• The club is "loaded" and parallel to the target line.

Stand in the mirror and practice getting into "the slot" at the top. It will make the downswing automatic.

Davis Love III gets into the slot on the 18th tee at the Pebble Beach National Pro-Am, en route to a one-stroke victory in 2003.

How to get set at the top
Think of the right arm forming a box

Width and extension are important for a powerful, repetitive golf swing. Maximize your power by imagining a box at the top of the swing.

The bottom and side of this box are formed by the right upper arm and the forearm, with a 90-degree angle at the elbow. The top of the box is created by the clubshaft, set at 90 degrees to the forearm.

This image encourages the right arm to swing into a good supporting position, with a full wrist cock. **The box image, plus a full shoulder turn, will** **help create a wide yet compact backswing.**

If you lose the box by letting your left forearm and upper arm collapse or by losing your grip at the top, you'll end up with a weak, noncoiled backswing. This will result in poor contact, lack of distance and off-line shots.

To practice the box sensation, swing back with just your right arm while your left hand is balanced on a club.

A solid right-arm position at the top provides width and support for the swing.

Maximize torque
How to store more power

The winding and unwinding process, **in which the hips and abdominal muscles move toward the target as the upper body completes the backswing,** provides a great deal of energy to the swing. You lose power when you start down with the upper and lower body moving together and throw the club from the top.

Try this: Get down on your knees and place a club behind your shoulders. Turn back and then start forward with a short movement of your hips and abs as you resist the urge to unwind the shoulders too early. You'll feel how powerful real torque is.

Torque, or torsion (not to be confused with tension), is required to hit solid shots.

Learn to add lag
A proper 'cast' boosts clubhead speed

Think of how you cast with a fishing rod: You swing the rod back over your shoulder, fully setting your wrist. As your arm brings the rod forward, your wrist not only maintains that angle, but also adds to it before snapping forward.

That's the motion you want to achieve from the top of the swing. Just as the tip of your fishing rod lags behind your hands as you cast, so should your clubhead on the downswing. Instead of throwing the club from the top by unhinging your wrists imme- diately, **add lag by sharpening the angle created by the club- shaft and forearms.** The clubhead catches up with the hands only as it speeds through the impact zone.

Many golfers waste power by unhinging their wrists too early from the top. You can increase your clubhead speed by cocking and uncocking your wrists correctly.

PAUL LIPP

The right elbow supports the club . . .
How to guide the club onto the correct plane

A common cause of slicing is the failure to support the club with the right elbow at the top of the swing. The result is that you lack coil and initiate the downswing with an over-the-top move with the shoulders, which sets the club on a downswing plane that's too steep.

Maintaining control of the right elbow helps support the club at the top and allows the swing to feel more wound up and compact. That stronger position promotes a first move down in which **the right elbow leads the hands and allows the right shoulder to move down instead of out.** The clubshaft can then approach the ball on a shallower plane, versus a too-steep, outside-to-in motion.

STEP 1

The right-arm-only drill can help turn a slicer's swing into a draw.

. . . And leads on the way down
Approach the ball on a shallow plane

The right-arm-only drill, which I'm demonstrating on these pages, allows you to feel the more-rounded inside motion necessary for the clubhead to approach the ball on a flatter plane.

Start by taking hold of the club—a middle iron works best—using only your right hand. Choke down on the grip for better control. Set the club in an at-the-top position in which your right arm is folded and your elbow is pointing toward the ground. Now swing so the right elbow works down toward the right hip.

When you move on to making conventional two-handed swings, **you should feel the clubhead trailing behind your hands,** which, with a fuller release, will produce a draw.

STEP 2

A common cause of slicing is the failure to support the club with the right elbow at the top of the swing. The result is a steep, over-the-top move coming down.

Maintain width on the downswing
Give your hands and arms room to swing down

When we talk of width, we're talking about the radius of your swing, how the clubhead travels in a circle around your body. Loss of width in the downswing drains power and affects accuracy.

Use the split-hands drill to help you maintain width where it counts: on the way down. Grip the club with your hands an inch apart and swing to the top. Now swing down, **allowing your left shoulder to move away from your chin.** At the same time, feel your right arm straightening slightly, the elbow clear of the right hip, while retaining the angle at your right wrist.

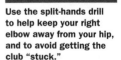

Use the split-hands drill to help keep your right elbow away from your hip, and to avoid getting the club "stuck."

How to speed up your arm swing
Whip it down to improve your timing and boost power

It's a simple equation: Greater clubhead speed equals more distance. One surefire way to boost clubhead speed is to speed up the arm swing. This is true for the higher-handicapper, who tends decelerate the arm swing in an effort to steer the ball; it's also true for the better player, whose hip turn and body rotation often outraces the hands and arms swinging down.

Try this drill: Hold a club upside down and practice whipping it down to where the clubshaft is parallel to the ground. Keep the lower body fairly passive as you **focus on hearing the "whoosh" of the clubshaft.**

A free arm-swing is important for width on the downswing and maximizes acceleration through impact.

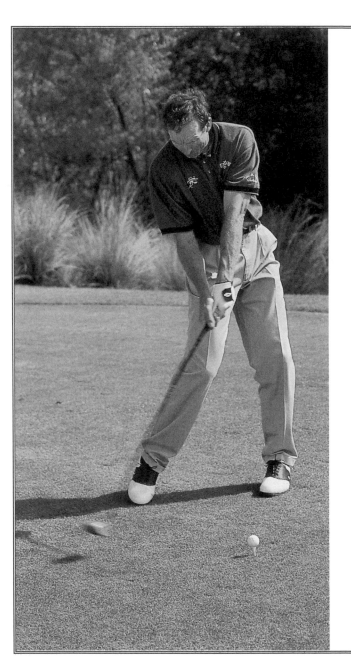

Hitting into a firm left side
Allow the right side to rotate hard

The "hit" in golf starts when the hands drop below the waist, and it's here where the lower body assumes a more active, aggressive role. **As your hips and upper body unwind through impact, your left leg needs to be firming or posting up.**

Try the left-foot-in drill I'm demonstrating at left to improve acceleration of the right side against a firm left side. Turning your left foot slightly inward at address promotes a more complete uncoiling of the right side and will reduce any tendency to slide your lower body through impact.

Use the left-foot-in drill to keep from sliding your lower body through impact.

'Post up' through impact

Straighten the left leg and arm

Ernie Els' impact position here is a classic image for a solid drive: **Hitting into a firm left side—left leg straight, left arm straight.**

Too many players collapse the left leg, or slide the lower body through the impact area, leaving them nothing to hit into.

Ernie's swing thought for this key position is to think of "hitting into" his left thigh. The centrifugal force created by his arm swing allows him to whip the club through impact, extending it down the target line before his turning body pulls his arms and clubs to the right. It's a move shared by all great power hitters.

The resistance a firm left side creates will allow you to whip the club through impact and extend your arms outward and away from your body, like a hammer thrower releases the hammer.

Keep your head behind the ball
Stay back to launch your drives

Impact is the most dynamic position in the swing. Here's a list of some of the key attributes:

• Your head is behind the ball;
• Your spine is angled to the right, away from the target;
• Your shoulders are more open to the target than they were at address; the hips even more open, about 45 degrees;
• The left arm is tight against the chest;

• Your right shoulder is tilted lower than your left;
• Your hands are more forward than the clubhead;
• The back of the left wrist is flat, with the wrists raised from their address position;
• The right knee points in, with the right foot rolled inward, up on the toes.

Model this impact position for a few seconds—then take that feeling to the tee.

Keeping your head behind the ball and your spine angled to the right promotes a free-wheeling release of the club.

Pop the balloon for more power
The right knee 'kicks in'

Many players fail to utilize the power in their legs. Through impact, it's common to see the right foot remain planted, the right knee failing to drive toward the target. This lack of lower-body movement prevents the necessary weight transfer from taking place.

Imagine a balloon between your knees at address. As you swing back, keep the balloon firmly in place. You want to maintain resistance in your legs as you maximize the coil.

As the clubhead nears impact, "pop the balloon" by driving the right knee toward the left knee. This imagery will allow you to clear the hips as your weight shifts onto the left leg.

Through impact, drive your right knee toward your left. This ensures the proper weight transfer and results in greater clubhead speed.

Maximize your speed at impact
Accelerate gradually on the way down

One hallmark of the higher-handicapper's swing—particularly the slicer's—is the tendency to be too aggressive at the start of the downswing. Slicers just want to kill the ball. Unfortunately, "hitting from the top" usually leads not to more power but less.

When the change of direction from backswing to downswing is too violent, problems arise. One is that the club often is thrust outside the ideal downswing plane, which leads to an "over the top" slice. Another is that the wrists uncock too early, which leads to a power-draining early release.

Forget the impulse to hit at the ball from the top. Accelerate gradually on the way down. At the point of impact, sense that you're exhaling as you **unleash the clubhead through the ball**—just as a black belt would when chopping a block of wood in two.

Hit through the ball just as a black belt chops a block of wood in two—with the greatest force applied right at impact.

Crack
the whip
How to release
the club

Of all the aspects of Vijay Singh's swing—his grace and flow, his huge turn and body rotation, his ball control—the one thing that grabs my attention is his release of the club through impact. As you can see in the photo here, Singh's right hand comes almost off the grip just after impact.

Is this a position the average golfer should try to emulate? Strictly speaking, no. But what it shows is the tremendous acceleration and free-wheeling move of the clubhead as the hands slow down.

Most golfers tighten up through impact, trying to over-control the club. Instead, **lighten your grip pressure, relax your arms and let the clubhead fly,** just like you're cracking a whip.

If you really want to hit the ball solidly, learn to time your swing so that the clubhead reaches maximum speed at impact. Lighten your grip pressure, relax your arms and let the club fly with a free-wheeling release of the hands.

For more distance, think 'anchors away'
Extend your arms toward the target

Many high-handicappers hit *at* the ball, not *through* it. As a result, the left arm collapses, the club slows down and weak shots result.

The image of **tossing a boat anchor down the fairway gets the arms extended past the ball,** helping you accelerate and square the clubface at impact. Keep your arms relaxed and make sure that your head stays back as you swing the anchor down the middle of the fairway. Chances are, the ball will follow.

For more arm extension and a better release, think of tossing an anchor down the middle of the fairway as you swing through.

Keep your swing arc wide after impact
Maintain the triangle formed by your arms and shoulders

Through the hitting zone, centrifugal force should be pulling your arms out away from your body toward the target. Focus on keeping the triangle formed by your arms and shoulders intact. The aim is to **maintain the radius of your swing arc all the way through the hitting area.**

Charles Howell III's post-impact position

is a model to copy. His head is back, his posture mirrors the position established at address, and his arms and club are fully extended. See the line formed by his left arm and shaft? Perfect.

Note his full release, the right forearm and hand over the left. There's no need to consciously manipulate the hands to release the club.

The turning of your body controls the release of the club. There is no need for any conscious crossing over of your hands in order to square the clubface.

Release your right side

Shift your weight fully to the left side

Acommon fault among amateurs is to finish the swing with too much weight on the right side. It's the result of a lack of body motion and an inhibited arm swing.

To swing with power, **the right side of the body must rotate all the way through.** As Ernie Els exhibits here in his full and balanced follow-through, your weight should be almost fully on your left foot; you want to feel as though you could step toward the target with your right foot.

Ernie Els shows great balance and extension; his right shoulder points to the target, and his weight is fully on his left foot.

Finish in balance, facing the target
How to achieve the ultimate follow-through position

Not many golfers can duplicate the wraparound finish of Michelle Wie. For that you need the flexibility of a teen, I'm afraid. But the pose Michelle strikes here is largely a look shared by all good golfers, and is a finish position well worth emulating.

Make practice swings in which you swing back to the top. **Hold the position for several seconds.** Then swing through so that the club nearly hits you in the back. Recoil it back somewhat, then hold the pose for several more seconds.

You should be facing the target, in balance, with your weight largely on your left foot.

Your finish may not be as pretty as this picture, but your overall swing motion should be improved.

Most amateurs never complete their backswing, nor do they complete their finish. You'll improve your overall swing if you practice holding your finish for a second or two.

From the Fairway:
Advance The Ball With More Consistency

If driving the ball off the tee is all about maximizing power, then advancing the ball from the fairway is about consistency. Solid ball-striking—especially when the ball is sitting on the ground—requires a full, rhythmic swing, with square contact that gets the ball airborne and flying straight to your target. The goal is to advance the ball all the way to the green or to put yourself in the best position to knock it close to the flag with your next shot. Let me show you how.

Consistency From the Fairway
Groove a repetitive swing motion

Most golfers who play regular-length courses and who hit the ball average distances will be faced with a lot of long shots toward the green. Add to that number if you also hit the occasional wayward drive off the tee and are forced to play a short shot back to safety.

The problem is, hitting longer-shafted, lower-lofted clubs with the ball sitting on the ground makes a lot of golfers nervous. Tension leads to a lack of rhythm and flow to the swing; the urge to help get the ball airborne only worsens the situation.

Today's new hybrid clubs—borrowing the best attributes of both the fairway wood and long iron—certainly can help improve your consistency from the fairway. But whether you're using a hybrid or fairway wood or long iron, the basic fundamentals remain in play. The proper ball position is crucial, as is a stable yet dynamic address position. **The key to better, more consistent contact from the fairway is in synchronizing the motions of your body and arms** to produce a full, free-flowing swing, back and through. In this chapter I'll show you how.

Annika Sorenstam exhibits peerless balance and synchronization, creating one of the most repetitive swings in golf.

51

Think 'sweep' on fairway woods
Create a shallow base to the swing arc

With a fairway wood you want **the sole of the club to skim the turf as it approaches the ball.** A helpful visual cue is to imagine you're brushing the ground with a broom, using a wide, sweeping motion. Use a light touch and sense the weight of the clubhead just as you would feel the broom's bristles sweeping across the ground.

Try also to sweep the clubhead away from the ball on the backswing. This will help you create good width early in your swing. And extend that sweeping action past impact.

You don't need to consciously "help" the ball into the air. Allow the loft of the club to do it for you.

Hitting the new hybrid clubs
Where to position the ball

Compared with a normal 3- or 4-iron, the forgiveness of a hybrid club is heaven. Though the designs and lofts vary from make to make, **the generally small, compact head, wide sole and low center of gravity of a hybrid make it easy to get the ball airborne.** Because there's so much more weight behind the ball, even if you hit slightly behind the ball with a hybrid, the club is going to swing on through.

Some players who have trouble getting a longer iron airborne play the ball farther forward in the stance and try to lift it with a flippy, scooping motion. A hybrid enables you to swing without any manipulation.

For the hybrid, your stance width should be the same as for a longer iron. Your ball position is forward of center, but not quite so forward as it would be for a tradtional fairway wood.

When hitting a hybrid from the fairway, position the ball slightly forward of center in your stance. Play it a touch farther back when using a hybrid from the rough.

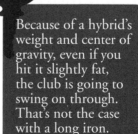

Because of a hybrid's weight and center of gravity, even if you hit it slightly fat, the club is going to swing on through. That's not the case with a long iron.

For square contact, improve your swing path
Keep the club outside the hands

Coming into the ball, the clubhead should travel along a path from slightly inside the target line. The clubhead moves down the target line through impact, then swings back to the inside as the body rotates to the finish.

Better golfers' problems tend to be a result of the club swinging too much in to out.

Keeping the clubhead more in front of, or outside, the hands on the downswing will alleviate this problem.

The farther the clubhead gets behind the hands coming down, the tougher it becomes to square the clubface consistently at impact.

Practice hitting balls with your right foot in line with your left heel. This encourages the right side to rotate around the left side of the body, which helps keep the clubhead outside the hands on a path that's more along the target line.

Use the right-foot-back drill to help release the right side and route the club along the target line.

Keep the club on line
'Bowl' your shots
down the fairway

To picture the proper movement of the right shoulder into and through impact, think of how you would roll a bowling ball: Your right shoulder works under and through as you throw the ball down the lane.

That's what you want to do with the golf swing. By contrast, **in the typical slicer's swing, the right shoulder moves up and out or "over the top,"** forcing the arms to re-route the club outside the target line.

To swing the club on line and with more power, keep your right hip, arm and shoulder in line, working the right shoulder down and through.

PAUL LIPP

To swing the club on line and with more power, keep your right hip, arm and shoulder in line, working the right shoulder down and through.

Feel how the arms and body blend

Get in sync for more consistent fairway shots

Practice the swing motion without a club to improve how to blend the turning body and the swinging of the arms and hands.

The two big components in the swing—the turning body and the swinging of the arms, hands and club—must be synchronized, especially through impact. If the body gets too far ahead of the club or the club outraces the body on the downswing, power and consistency will be lost. **Call it timing or rhythm or sequencing, this prerequisite is the reason you can feel like you own your swing one day, and can't find it the next.** To feel how the body and arms blend together, practice

the no-club drill I'm demonstrating above. Here's how:
• Take your address position, placing your left hand behind your right.
• Move your arms and torso as though taking a normal backswing, using your right arm to help maintain width and create torque.
• "Swing" your arms down, keeping your lower body stable; use your thumbs to trace your downswing plane.
• Sync up your rotating body with a free-wheeling release of your arms to a balanced finish.

Synchronizing your swing is only one aspect of consistency. You also need to make sure that your swing is on plane. If it's too steep or too flat, or if you fan the club open or keep it too shut going back, you have to make compensations on the downswing.

Hitting More Greens:
Accurate Iron Play

Irons are direction clubs, not distance clubs. With the driver, you're creating a swing that produces a level, or slightly upward, blow. With your irons, the swing you need is a slightly descending strike, the clubhead making contact with the ball, then the turf. In this chapter, I'll show you how to make solid contact with greater consistency, from the longer irons to the scoring clubs.

Accurate Iron Play
Keep your swing simple and efficient

The best iron swings, whether we're talking about a Ben Hogan of a past generation or a Nick Price of the modern era, are simple, efficient and ultra-repetitive, with no wasted motion.

Solid fundamentals are the foundation and allow the moving parts of the swing to blend in rhythm and complete synchronization.

Everybody can learn from Nick Price, seen here hitting a short iron. An athletic, dynamic setup allows him to make a compact, fully coiled backswing over a stable lower body. Note how he's kept the flex in his right knee at the top of his backswing and maintained his spine angle.

Many players straighten up as they swing back or dip the left shoulder.

Price's top-of-swing position allows him to get the club on the correct plane on the downswing, returning the club at impact to the identical position it was in at address. **It's the secret to his consistency and great ball-striking.**

Nick may have a quick tempo to his swing, but it suits his temperament, in much the same way Ernie Els' easygoing personality suits his longer, more languid swing. The key is that Nick swings at the same pace every time, with every club. He calls it a "quiet" swing, but it speaks volumes.

A compact, aggressive swing has made Nick Price one of the game's all-time best ball-strikers, especially with his middle irons.

Keep your hands soft, your arms relaxed
Stay loose at address

The more relaxed and in balance your body is at address, the more rhythmic your swing will be. And better rhythm translates directly to more consistency and power.

They don't call Ernie Els the "Big Easy" without reason. Notice here how soft his hands and arms appear as he sets up to the ball with his 5-iron.

To reduce tension at address, try this simple drill: Grip a club normally and raise it in front of you so the clubshaft is parallel to the ground. **You should be able to sense the weight of the clubhead in your hands.**

If you can't, you're keeping too much tension in your shoulders, arms and hands.

Feel like your arms are soft in front of you. Stand tall, with your chin up to reduce tension in your shoulders, your weight centered over the balls of your feet. Feel, too, a sense of liveliness in your feet and legs. You're now ready to begin the swing in balance and with better tempo.

Relaxed hands and arms are a source of power for Ernie Els, the epitome of "swing easy, hit hard."

How to grip it for better feel
'Thread the needle' for more control

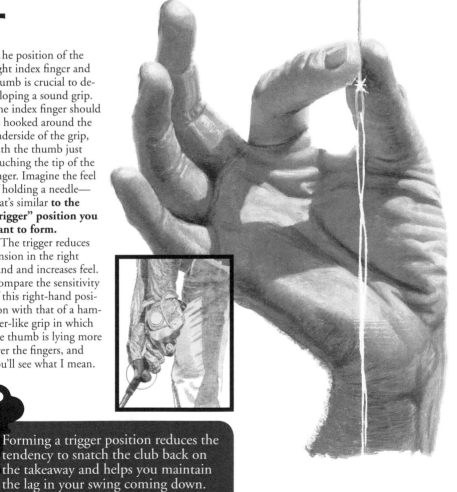

The position of the right index finger and thumb is crucial to developing a sound grip. The index finger should be hooked around the underside of the grip, with the thumb just touching the tip of the finger. Imagine the feel of holding a needle—that's similar **to the "trigger" position you want to form.**

The trigger reduces tension in the right hand and increases feel. Compare the sensitivity of this right-hand position with that of a hammer-like grip in which the thumb is lying more over the fingers, and you'll see what I mean.

Forming a trigger position reduces the tendency to snatch the club back on the takeaway and helps you maintain the lag in your swing coming down.

Widen your swing arc
'Start the mower' to start the swing

PAUL LIPP

To create width in the backswing, **the right arm needs freedom to move back and up into the proper position at the top.**

Think of how you fire up a lawn mower: Without any thought you simply draw the cord back with a free-flowing motion that begins with the right hand, then the right elbow, followed by the shoulder. This image helps you synchronize your body action with your arm movement in your golf swing.

A lot of golfers "tuck" their right elbow and get very narrow on the backswing. Such a move can cause numerous swing faults, including an outside-in path on the downswing, which obviously will decrease accuracy and power.

Thinking of the lawn mower move will add coil and a good weight transfer to your backswing, providing more power as well as a downswing path from the inside.

"Pull the cord" to help put the right arm in the proper position at the top of the swing.

Improve your takeaway
Keep the clubhead outside the hands

To prevent an early turn of the body and to promote a better line to the takeaway, practice the initial move away from the ball while holding a club under your arms. This gives you an awareness of **your shoulders slightly tilting as the left shoulder turns under the chin.** Note that my shoulders have turned back more than my hips and my knees have pretty much maintained the same position they had at the start, the left knee moving slightly inward as I wind back. The club should remain outside your hands at this stage of the swing.

Many high-handicappers start their swings by snatching the clubhead away too quickly. Instead, think of moving the grip end of the club first.

Get into the slot at the top
Swing up on a slightly steepening

Ben Hogan imagined the ideal backswing plane as a pane of glass extending from the ball through the player's neck. In my experience, the image that Hogan used tends to set the golfer's hands too far around and behind the chest. This can lead you to simply lift your arms to complete the backswing, arriving in a weak, noncoiled position at the top.

A more helpful image, I feel, shows a golfer standing within a curved sheet of glass. This is ideal for the backswing, because **the curve in the glass represents the slight, gradual steepening of the plane, which leads to an on-plane downswing.**

Keeping your hands more in front of your chest allows you to move from the halfway-back position up to the perfect slot at the top simply by completing your shoulder turn— the ideal way to complete the backswing.

Use this image of a concave pane of glass to help you swing the club up on a slightly steepening plane.

Keep your hands in front of your chest
How to prevent an early turn

The problem I see with many golfers is that they turn the body too early on the backswing, a move that causes the hands to pull the club too far inside the target line. From this flat position all they can do is lift the club to the top with the arms to finish the backswing.

Halfway back, **the hands should remain in front of the chest with the shaft pointing just inside the ball-target line,** an in-sync, on-plane position Charles Howell III demonstrates at right. From here the arms and body will complete the backswing in sync.

An independent motion of the hands and arms results in a lack of coil and the club being thrown from the top or being released too early—swing flaws typically seen with slicers. Good synchronization starts immediately.

Get in sync . . .
How Vijay stays connected

**Vijay Singh's extraordi-
nary work ethic and talent
have kept him on top of
his game into his 40s.**

What's the key to
Vijay Singh's consisten-
cy? Without question,
it's his repetition, honed
by years of diligent
practice.

Being a big man and
having a swing with
plenty of motion—big
hip turn, long arm
swing, lots of hand ac-
tion through impact—
it's imperative that he
has good rhythm and
good syncronization
between his arms and
torso.

To encourage this
connection, **Vijay
practices with a glove
under his left arm and
keeps it there through
the swing.** The fact
that Vijay can complete
a full backswing with
full extension of the
left arm and a free right
elbow while retaining
the glove under his left
arm shows his amazing
flexibility.

. . . With half swings
Here's a drill for you, too

Since few golfers are blessed with Vijay Singh's suppleness, most players should focus on hitting short shots with only a half swing **to sense the link or connection between the arms and body.**

Tuck a towel under your arms. Now take half swings with a pitching wedge without dropping the towel. (During the hickory-shaft era, the big thing in golf instruction was to put a handkerchief under the right arm to help keep control of the whippy-shafted clubs. Jack Nicklaus changed that line of thinking for good when he came on the scene displaying his famous "flying" right elbow.) As your practice swings with the towel get longer in both directions, the towel will fall out. Let it—remember, you're focusing on making half swings to sense the connection as you get to the top.

As the backswing completes with the club, so it basically completes with the body.

Shorten your swing for more control
Create width by fully setting the club

There's no reason to swing the club past horizontal at the top. It's inefficient and leads to inconsistent contact.

Here's a way to eliminate the overswing for better control while creating the width you need for power.

Imagine standing with your back against a small doorway. As you swing the club back, think of pushing your hands up into one corner of the door frame while the club lies across the top.

Keep your left arm comfortably straight, while creating **as wide a backswing arc as possible.** Your right arm should be bent about 90 degrees and your wrists fully cocked.

Maximize your body coil for power while having a relatively short arm swing for control.

Remember to pause at the top

Why rush? The ball's not going anywhere

Novice golfers typically assume that staying in control means less movement. And the less movement they have, the better their chance of hitting the ball. So they keep their heads still and swing the club primarily with their arms. The result is an incomplete body turn, no width and an ax-like chop with the arms at the ball.

The only time in the swing you want to think "less movement" is as you complete the backswing. Pause at the top. **Feel a good, strong position, where you're fully wound up and coiled,** like Charles Howell is here. You're now ready to swing your arms down from the top as your body uncoils.

Focusing on "the hit" leads to such faults as an armsy swing, lack of coil and poor weight transfer. Don't be in a rush to start down before you've completed your backswing.

Maximize your leverage
Finish you coil as you step into the shot

When you're throwing a baseball or hitting a golf ball, as you wind up with the upper torso away from the target, you are at the same time starting to uncoil toward the target with your body.

Think of how a pitcher moves his left foot toward home plate as his arm is still reaching back. **In golf, you also want the lower left side—the left knee and hip—initiating the downswing even while the club is being swung back.**

This motion increases the leverage in the swing and is seen in all solid ball-strikers.

"Step into" the down-swing as you maximize your coil, just as a pitcher rears back to throw a baseball.

Make a better weight transfer
Your body rotates around two points

Power and consistency comes from turning your weight around two axis points. **On the backswing, the body rotates around an axis roughly in line with the inside of your right foot.**

Ingrain the feeling with the drill I'm demonstrating above: Hold a club in front of you to practice shifting your weight around your right side as you swing to the top. For the through-swing move, hold the club with your right hand. Starting from just before impact, swing your left arm and turn through, shifting your weight around a point in line with the inside of your left foot.

Throwing a baseball echoes what should be happening dynamically in the golf swing, particularly the transition from the backswing to the downswing. This image puts you in a position from which you can release your entire right side into the ball.

Improve your lag position
Think 'hands low, clubhead high'

Sergio Garcia probably has more lag than any other world-class player, a position he demonstrates in the photo here. This so-called late hit or **lag position is a prerequisite for releasing the clubhead at maximum speed through impact.**

Flexible wrists certainly help, and the fact that Garcia has a fairly late set on the backswing contributes as well. Although it can be dangerous to try to put the club in this position, a good image for improving your lag is "hands low and clubhead high" coming into impact. Practicing with the grip leading the clubhead in this way could really help your ball striking.

Sergio Garcia keeps his hands low and clubhead high before whipping the clubhead through impact.

How to increase your wrist cock
Know the value of 'the lag'

Many golfers lose much of the power they've created on the way back by uncocking their wrists too early on the way down.

To maximize your clubhead speed, delay the uncocking of the wrists until just before impact. Learn to increase your clubhead lag with this simple drill: Hold the fingers of your right hand in a "cocked" position as you slowly swing your arms down. **As you approach the impact position, release the fingers to snap the right hand forward.** That's the feeling you want as you whip the club through the ball.

To maximize your clubhead speed and improve your ball striking, delay the uncocking of the wrists until just before impact.

Hammer your short irons
Swing down and through

For solid iron shots, especially with the short irons, you've got to make sure you descend down and through the ball. It's like a hammer pounding a nail into a block of wood. **You want to drive the clubhead into the back of the ball.**

Strike the ball with a descending blow, with the clubhead making contact with the ball, then the turf. That will give you a sensation of pounding the ball like a nail into the turf, as opposed to scooping or trying to lift the ball into the air.

With your irons, you want to make contact with a descending blow, hitting down and through.

How to hit your irons straighter
'Cover' the ball with the clubface

Golfers with directional problems–slicers and pullers—contact the ball with the clubface open, aiming to the right of the target.

To counter this fault, practice hitting shots in which you try to close the clubface well before impact. The feel you want is that **the clubface is** **actually looking at the ball about two feet before impact.** Closing the clubface this early in the downswing prevents a last-gasp, flippy, handsy move at impact to try to get the clubface square. With a little practice, this feeling will result in a straighter, more penetrating ball flight.

Tired of yelling, "Fore, right!"? Practice hitting iron shots in which you try to close the clubface well before impact.

Deliver your power at the right time
Give your arms room to swing through

To hit solid shots, the clubhead needs to accelerate along the target line through impact, the clubface square to that line. The club's greatest speed, however, comes when it approaches the ball on a wide, rounded arc, continuing on that arc after impact.

In the photo at left, Ernie Els demonstrates the importance of **maintaining the proper body angles to allow the hands and arms to swing through at maximum speed,** on the correct plane and in sync with the turning body.

Through impact, Ernie keeps his spine angle the same as it was at address. He's made a complete weight transfer to his left side as his body opens and rotates to the left. This full release of the body prevents the club from getting "stuck" behind him, squares the clubface naturally and allows him to extend his arms fully for maximum clubhead speed when it matters most: right at impact.

Maintaining the proper body angles allows Ernie Els to return the club on plane through impact.

How to whip the club through impact
Use centrifugal force like a water-skier

Think of a boat pulling a water-skier. As the boat makes a turn, the skier veers away on a curved arc at tremendous speed. The boat is not increasing its speed, but through centrifugal force the skier certainly is.

That's a great image for golfers. As your body (the boat) rotates to the left, **your arms (the tow rope) and** **the clubhead (the skier) accelerate on a rounded inside path.**

It's important to keep your body (the boat) moving and rotating all the way to the finish. If the boat stops, the rope slackens and the skier sinks. In other words, the arms collapse and the clubhead decelerates.

As your body and hands work left through impact, the clubhead speeds up, just as a skier accelerates behind a turning boat. Centrifugal force at work.

Learn to hit down and through . . .

How to improve your contact

For crisp shots, you've got to learn to hit down on the ball. One of the best ways to do this is to practice on a downslope. Use a middle iron and select a lie in which your forward foot is a couple of inches below your rear foot. The ball should be on the same incline— not appreciably above or below your feet.

Set your shoulders parallel with the slope, the ball back a bit from normal. Use two clubs to form a "T," as I'm doing here, to monitor your shoulder line and ball position. Your spine angle should lean toward the target. Players who try to lift the ball in the air will typically tilt backward or upward, coming out of the shot.

Hitting down correctly on the ball with an iron leads to good trajectory and backspin.

. . . By practicing from a downhill lie
Shift your weight to your front leg coming down

As you hit shots from a downslope, focus on maintaining the spine angle established at address and shifting your weight to your front leg as you swing down.

Feel as if your right thigh is more on top of the ball through impact. This allows your hands to be forward, helping create clubhead lag and a descending blow.

To get the ball airborne, many golfers think they have to "get under it." Instead, learn to strike the ball with a descending blow, and trust the loft of the clubhead to get the ball up in the air.

Extend for a solid shot
Keep your head behind the ball

Two common flaws in the impact position of high-handicappers occur when the head moves forward and the left arm bends and flares out—the chicken-wing finish. Shingo Katayama exhibits the proper form in both regards here. Note how he keeps his chin behind the ball well after impact, with the upper part of his left arm snug against his chest with the whole arm extended.

Keep this post-impact position in mind as you swing through the ball, focusing on **keeping your head back and maintaining the triangle formed by the arms and shoulders.**

Follow Shingo Katayama's simple rule: Head back and extend through for a solid shot.

How to release the club

The left arm extends and rotates

To get a better idea of the proper sequence of motions involved in the release, think of how you toss out a handful of chicken feed left-handed. You wouldn't just flick your wrist, you'd use the whole arm and wrist together in such a way that the left arm rotates and allows you to cast the chicken feed across a wide swath.

That's the same flowing motion you want through impact. **The left hand is not buckled, but in firm control of the clubface.** The arms extend in front of the turning body, with the left arm rotating so the left palm faces upward halfway into the follow-through.

To avoid a "chicken-wing" finish, think "chicken feed," releasing the club through impact just as you would cast chicken feed with your left hand.

Finish your swing in balance
Think 'up on your right toe'

Finishing your swing in balance isn't your ultimate goal, but it is proof you've been in balance when it really counts: through impact.

The follow-through position Nick Price strikes here shows that he's shifted his weight fully to his left side, with only his right toe on the ground. His right shoulder is slightly lower than and closer to the target than his left. This finish position demonstrates that he's **rotated right through the shot by clearing his left side and firing his right.**

Copy Price's position to avoid two common flaws: an excessive lateral slide of the lower body through impact or a falling-back motion of the upper body.

As Nick Price's longevity attests, a key benefit of a balanced swing is in reducing stress on the back.

Pack a punch on your follow-through

Learn how to release the right side

To make the most of the power generated on the downswing, you must release the right side fully toward the target through impact all the way to the finish.

The feeling is very much like a boxer throwing a punch. When a boxer delivers a blow, he forcefully shifts his weight forward as he extends his right arm and shoulder toward the target. Finish your swing with the same knockout punch. **Fire through the ball by releasing your right side.**

Rotate your body all the way through the shot, so that your right shoulder is pointing toward the target at the completion of the follow-through.

Rotate your body all the way through, so that your right shoulder is pointing toward the target at the completion of the follow-through.

SWING SEQUENCES

MICHELLE WIE
Study Michelle's solid setup, her beautiful angles
at the top of the swing and perfect timing through impact.

CHARLES HOWELL, III
How does this slim young man hit his drives so far?
With tremendous coil, leverage and great balance.

NICK PRICE
Nick's secret to hitting irons consistently well:
Eliminate as many moving parts as possible.

ERNIE ELS
The Big Easy shows you how to splash the ball
out of the bunker along with the sand.

**Tower of power:
Michelle Wie uses
a solid foundation
to support her
wide swing arc
and full-body coil.**

Straight-shooter: Charles Howell keeps the club on plane and in perfect position throughout the swing.

Mr. Consistency: A simple, repetitive and efficient swing gives Nick Price pinpoint control with his irons.

Making a splash: Ernie Els exhibits textbook form in making the swing you need to knock it close from the sand.

Around the Green:
Saving Strokes

Because you haven't the time to make compensations in the short chipping and pitching motions, they demand more exactness than the full swing. ⬤ Brute strength and clubhead speed aren't the goals; touch and feel are. ⬤ The good news: With practice and sound fundamentals, virtually any golfer can possess a solid short game. ⬤ And if you can get your technique correct on the short chip or pitch, it will not only save you strokes, it will help your long game as well.

Saving strokes around the green

A good short game is all about feel. Here's how to get it

The chip shot requires the shortest of strokes, with minimal hand and little body action, which makes a sound setup crucial to producing a solid result. In this chapter, I'll show you how to position yourself for consistent, crisp contact.

It's equally important that when you hit pitch shots, your hands don't get overly active. However, as these shots get longer, the body plays a bigger role, as you can see here with Jim Furyk. On wedge shots he uses his lower body to help propel the club through the ball. Working "under" the ball allows Furyk's right shoulder to move almost on the same line as his right knee, helping keep the clubface square through impact. There's no scooping or crossing over motion with his hands, and the clubface never closes.

With the turning chest and lower body propelling the shot and the hands remaining passive, Furyk's wedge play is a good model for the average player to copy.

Read on for more short-game drills and tour-player examples to learn from.

When hitting wedge shots, Jim Furyk uses his lower body to propel the club. It's a great way to control the pace of the swing.

Visualize the shot you need
How to develop better touch and feel

All great short-game players have great imagination around the green. To become more creative in visualizing your options and to develop better judgment on shot selection, practice tossing balls underhanded to the hole. Experiment with different speeds and trajectories, from high and soft to low and running. **Notice which trajectory you need, and where you have to land the ball, to allow you to get it close to the hole.** Use the results as a guideline to select the club and the type of shot that would give you the same results.

Tossing balls underhanded is Greg Norman's favorite greenside exercise—and he is a wonderful exponent of the short game.

'Toss the ball' to control distance

Use the right hand to help square the clubface

Tossing a ball under-handed is more than a good concept to help develop your short-game creativity; it's also a fitting image to help you improve your short-game mechan-ics. As you would do pitching a softball, **on a pitch shot the right hand faces up through impact,** under the left hand. You're not trying to scoop the ball; the right hand mirrors the clubface, and keeping the palm face up through impact helps keep the clubface square, with the proper loft. The clubface doesn't close until well into the finish of the swing.

When hitting pitch shots, the clubface stays square to the target line. There's no crossover with the hands.

Setup for a descending blow
'Jack up' your right side

Agood chipping stroke requires you to nip the ball off the turf with a slight descending blow.

To help you set up properly, imagine that a tiny car jack has raised your right heel off the ground. This image will help you **lean more of your weight onto your left side** and encourage your hands to be ahead of the ball at impact.

Just position the ball back in your stance and the club will automatically swing up and down, striking the ball on the descent.

Shift more weight to your left side to promote a crisp, descending strike on chip shots.

How to hit crisp chips
Set up so the low point of the swing is ahead of the ball

The idea of picking up the right heel is so helpful in improving your chipping technique, I often tell golfers to practice chipping while standing on the left foot only.

When you pick the back foot up, **it encourages your chest to move forward of the ball,** which means that your impact point—the low point of your swing arc—is also slightly forward of the ball. Standing on the front foot helps eliminate excessive lower-body motion. And it focuses you on feeling that the left hand leads the clubhead, so you can't flip at the ball. That's important for solidly struck chip shots.

Poor chippers set up with too much weight on the right side and make a wristy, upward strike. Good chippers keep their hands ahead of the ball.

To hit soft pitches . . .
The right elbow needs to lead

The soft pitch shot, where the ball lands on the green with very little roll, is an important part of the short-game repertoire. To execute it, **swing the club smoothly and clip the ball off the grass.** This is not a shot in which you swing down steeply and take a big divot or try to lift the ball in the air with an upward, scooping motion of the wrists. I recommend using your sand or lob wedge, with a right-arm motion I'll describe at right.

The right elbow leads the downswing to prevent the club from digging in.

... Learn to clip the ball

The palm opens, then releases

Practice a pitching movement with a sand wedge in which the right elbow leads the downswing so **the back of the club, which sits lower than the leading edge (known as the bounce) makes contact with the turf at the proper angle.** Imagine the palm of your right hand is the clubface; ingrain the feel of the palm opening on the backswing and releasing through impact. The bounce prevents the club from digging in and allows it to skim the grass under the ball.

Imagine the palm of your right hand is the clubface. This will help you understand how the face opens on the backswing and releases through impact.

Keep the left wrist firm
For better chips, reduce your hand action

Faced with a delicate chip from just off the green, many players get tense and lose rhythm. They jerk the club back and then flip the hands at it as they try to scoop the ball in the air.

If this sounds like you, try this drill: Start with the club a short distance behind the ball—relaxed arms, minimal wrist cock, your weight favoring the left foot. From here, move the clubhead back a few inches with a little turn, then turn back toward the target, **keeping your left wrist firm.** The result will be a solid clip of the ball off the turf—less hands and more consistency.

For a more rhythmic chipping stroke through the ball, use a little body turn as you keep your hands ahead of the clubhead.

Your body is the engine of the swing

Turn your torso even on the shortest of swings

On chips and pitches, make sure the engine of the swing is your chest, not your hands. If your chest stays still while your hands move—well, that's when you get flippy with your hands and end up hitting the ball fat or thin.

To keep your hands in the proper relation with your chest, imagine a rope connecting the chest to the top of the club. Keep that rope taut as your torso turns back and through and your hands remain fairly passive. That will help you **maintain a constant width to your swing** so you can hit the ball crisply.

On chip shots and short pitches, the hands must stay ahead of the clubhead as you turn through. If your chest stays still while your hands move, that's when you get flippy with your hands and hit the ball fat or thin.

How to dial in distance

Learn to gauge the speed of your body turn

The usual cause of poor distance control on pitches is overuse of the hands and arms. **Let the speed that you rotate your body control the distance of the shot.**

In other words, put your swing on an imaginary speedometer. For a short swing—say, 20 yards—swing 20 miles per hour. For a long shot—say, 60 yards—swing 60 mph.

You'll automatically take a longer swing for longer shots and a shorter swing for shorter shots, but all you should think about is rotational speed. Just put in some practice to calibrate your speedometer.

A narrow stance with your weight favoring your left leg is ideal. Let the speed of your body rotation determine your distance.

Accelerate through impact
How to hit the flop like Phil Mickelson

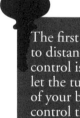

The high flop is a Phil Mickelson trademark. He takes a full, slow swing, sliding his lofted wedge under the ball. The ball flies out very high, goes a short distance and stops dead when it lands. You can see here how full Phil's swing is, yet the ball is still in the picture.

Most golfers should attempt this shot only if there is a cushion of grass under the ball. **The backswing has to be long and slow to allow the weight of the clubhead—preferably a 60-degree wedge—to propel the ball.** A common mistake is to swing too short and try to scoop the ball into the air. Accelerate through impact; decelerating is the kiss of death on this touch shot.

The first key to distance control is to let the turning of your body control the motion of the club. The arms are just along for the ride, not swinging independently.

Deep rough? Make a full, aggressive swing
Cushion your shots from greenside rough

PAUL LIEF

onto the green. It's like an explosion shot from sand. Open your stance and clubface, then with a smooth swing, contact the grass first to lift the ball up and out of the rough on a cushion of grass. The beauty of this image is that it allows you to make a fuller, more aggressive swing. You can feel free to create more clubhead speed because contacting the grass first will slow the clubhead down yet still allow you to propel the ball out of the rough. Flying on its cushion of grass, the ball will land softly and safely on the green.

For better control from greenside rough, visualize the grass behind and under the ball as a cushion. You're not trying to hit the ball, **your goal is to sweep the cushion up**

Pitching from thick rough is like an explosion shot from sand. Contact the grass first to lift the ball up on a cushion of grass.

How to chip with a hybrid
Scoot the ball just over the fringe

Want to save a lot of shots around the greens? Use a hybrid club to scoot the ball over the fringe and get it rolling like a putt.

Stand close to the ball so the shaft is more vertical, your eyes nearly over the ball. Play the ball more off your back foot. **This encourages a descending blow to trap the ball against the turf**—that's what allows it to shoot forward over the fringe.

Take the club back without much wrist set. If you break your wrists during the shot, you'll add too much loft to the club. Accelerate through, with your hands leading the club through impact. The ball will hop over the fringe, then roll like a putt. Todd Hamilton used this shot very effectively to win the British Open in 2004.

If you lack confidence in your chipping, use a hybrid club from off the green. There's a big margin for error compared to a chip shot with an iron.

Bunker Shots:
Get It Out,
Get It Close

Too many amateurs fear just getting out of a bunker, never mind getting the ball close to the hole. Basically, you need a similar length back-swing for all bunker shots, while aiming a couple of inches behind the ball with an open clubface and taking a shallow cut of sand as you swing through. My general rule for the finish: The length of the follow-through determines the length of the shot. Read on for more keys to better bunker play.

Bunker shots:
Get it out, get it close
Combine the right tools with the proper technique

In many ways, the shot from sand is the simplest in golf—though for many golfers this is not the case. You can use a specialized tool—the sand wedge—and are allowed more margin for error. The club doesn't contact the ball; you hit behind the ball to splash it out. Use these keys to improve your bunker play:

• Set up to the ball with a stance that's slightly open to the target.
• Open the clubface— it points slightly right of the target—then take your grip.
• Aim to hit a point in the sand a couple inches behind the ball.
• Swing back along your toe line, then swing down along the target line; think of the swing as a looping motion to the inside.
• Keep the clubface open at impact.

Getting the face into this position helps the heel of the club enter the sand first, and allows the bounce—the back edge of the bottom of the club is lower than the leading edge—to slide through the sand under the ball without too much resistance.

• The longer the follow-through, the more acceleration and the farther the ball goes.

On the pages that follow, I'll explain these simple keys in more detail.

Ernie Els exhibits the same fluid, easy tempo from the sand as he does on all shots.

105

Rotate the clubface open
'Balance a glass' on the way back

An open clubface on the way back—imagine balancing a glass on it—helps the club slide under the ball through impact.

To hit consistent bunker shots, the clubface needs to be open at impact, removing a shallow cut of sand from under the ball.

To keep the clubface from closing at impact, **rotate the clubface open so that you could almost balance a glass on the face.**

Getting the face into this position helps the heel of the club enter the sand first, enabling you to slide the club under the ball without too much resistance from the sand.

As it enters the sand a couple inches behind the ball, the open clubface with the heel leading—as opposed to the closed face with the heel digging—will allow you to control the amount of sand you take.

Accelerate through the sand
Control distance by adjusting the length of your swing

Just as it does on a shot from grass, decelerating the clubhead through impact leads to disaster from sand. You're not making contact with the ball, your intent is to slide the club through the sand under the ball.

Because of the resistance the sand creates, the general rule is that **to hit the ball the same distance from sand as you would from grass requires you to swing about three times more aggressively.**

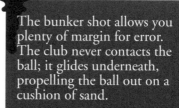

The bunker shot allows you plenty of margin for error. The club never contacts the ball; it glides underneath, propelling the ball out on a cushion of sand.

Swing back along your toe line . . .

Set your wrists fairly quickly

Many poor bunker players cut across the ball on an angle that's too steep, and as a result they bury the club in the sand, with the ball going nowhere. Learn to shallow out your swing so the club glides into the sand under the ball.

Open your stance and open the clubface as you set up to the ball. **Swing back along your toe line.** The clubhead stays outside the hands as you set your wrists fairly quickly. Keep your lower body stable as you swing back and start down.

The proper bunker swing is an "out-to-in" looping motion—just the opposite of the slicer's typical "in-and-over-the-top" swing.

... And down along the target line

Shallow out the downswing

On the downswing, feel as if you've got a slight looping action. Swing down along the target line, the clubhead traveling on a shallow, inside path to the ball. This encourages the heel of the clubhead to enter the sand first. **Your sand "divot" should be shallow and point toward the hole.** Accelerate through impact, listening for the "thump" of the bottom of the club splashing firmly through the sand.

Open your stance and swing the club back along your toe line, then swing down along the target line.

Use the right tool for the job
Let the loft and bounce of a sand wedge work for you

Let's talk equipment. No, this is not a commercial, though I imagine you'll be able to guess my brand of choice from the photo at left.

It's a tip about how **you can buy a better sand game.** Sand wedges come in a variety of designs, lofts and bounce angles. Choosing the club that's right for you depends on the type of course you play. Whether the bunkers are shallow or deep, and whether the sand is soft and fluffy or thin and hard will influence your choice. Check with your golf professional for advice on the best sand wedge for you.

The sole of the sand wedge (*near club*) is designed so that it will glide through the sand without digging in.

Keep the clubface open
Use your finish as a checkpoint

Here's a visual reminder I often give to students who are having difficulty with bunker shots. On the finish, swing the club to eye level. **If the clubface were a mirror, you would be able to see your reflection in it.** It's proof that you've kept the clubface open at impact and allowed the sand wedge to glide under the ball.

The key to success from greenside bunkers is to keep the clubface open throughout the swing. Closing the clubface through impact will cause it to dig into the sand, resulting in poor shots.

111

Keep your body quiet
Create a stable, balanced base

As Ernie Els shows here, the short bunker shot is a swing controlled by your arms, not your body.

When playing from sand, it's vital to create a stable base. Play the ball forward in your stance, and set your feet slightly wider than normal, opening your stance about 30 degrees in relation to the target. **Shuffle your feet into the sand for a firm footing, your weight evenly distributed, and flex your knees.** Stand slightly farther from the ball than normal, with your hands a bit lower, even with or slightly behind the ball. This position ensures good balance, effectively adds loft to the club and promotes a shallow arc to the swing.

As you swing through, feel that your right hand works under the left. This will help keep the clubface open through impact, popping the ball up quickly from the sand.

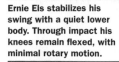

Ernie Els stabilizes his swing with a quiet lower body. Through impact his knees remain flexed, with minimal rotary motion.

Toss the sand to the hole

How to judge distance from greenside bunkers

Many golfers find it difficult to judge how much acceleration is needed to get the ball to the hole when hitting a greenside bunker shot. They have trouble accounting for how much the sand slows down the clubhead.

Think of throwing the *sand* to the hole. **Once you picture trying to toss the sand out of the bunker, you'll naturally release the clubhead more aggressively, as you should.**

Getting the sand out onto the green indicates that you have generated sufficient acceleration of the clubhead. Put another way, if you get the sand up close to the hole, you're probably going to get the ball there, too.

Practice without a ball. Splash the sand onto the green, taking a 'divot' six inches long and three inches wide. Then place a ball on the sand and hit about two inches behind it.

The longer the shot . . .

For short shots, swing to chest-high

One factor remains consistent on most greenside bunker shots from a regular lie: The amount of sand you take should be the same. Ideally, you want a thin slice of sand about the size of a dollar bill. **What differs, depending on the length of the shot, is the length of your follow-through.** This controls the force with which the ball is thrown with the sand onto the green. For shorter shots, finish with the club in front of your chest, as I'm doing in the first photo here.

For a short sand shot, finish with the club in front of your chest; for longer shots the hands finish higher.

114

...The longer the finish

Your hands finish higher on longer bunker shots

As your distance from the hole increases, so does **the pace of your swing through impact and into the follow-through.**

For standard shots, finish with your hands about head-high, as I'm demonstrating in the near photo at left.

For long shots from the sand, finish with a full arm swing and a full turn.

Practice this acceleration factor, and your distance control will quickly improve.

To control distance from the sand, make the same length backswing, but vary the length of your follow-through.

On the Green:
More One-putts,
No Three-putts

Although putting styles vary from golfer to golfer, all good putters share common traits. ● The most important one is the ability to repeat a stroke that starts the ball rolling true and on its intended line at good speed. ● This consistency can best be achieved by a shoulder-controlled, pendulum stroke, which prevents excessive body movement and hand action—the two flaws I see in poor putters. ● Want to hit your long putts closer and make more short ones? Read on.

More one-putts, no three-putts

Improve your tempo on long putts, your confidence on short putts

Putting is largely about personal preferences, whether you're talking about your choice in putter designs, the length of the putter or, increasingly, even the type of putting grip you use. **Although individual putting styles vary greatly, some traits are shared by all good putters.** These fundamental rules include:

• Follow a consistent routine as you determine the line of the putt and the stroke you'll need to hit the putt solidly on the intended line.

• Set up to the ball with your knees slightly flexed and your eyes over or slightly inside the ball and the target line.

• Keep the lower body stable and the head still.

• Swing the putter with the same steady tempo, whether you're stroking a three-foot putt or a 30-footer.

• On short putts, the putterface stays square to the target line as the putter swings straight back and straight through.

• As the putt gets longer, the putter travels on more of an arc, traveling slightly inside the target line on the back and forward swings.

• All good putters keep the putterface square to the target line through impact.

In this chapter I'll show you how to put these simple rules to use to improve your own putting game.

aron Baddeley's
putting routine is
quick, decisive
and never varies.
's made him
one of the best
putters on the
GA Tour.

Think 'tick-tock' to control distance
Follow the same two-beat tempo on all putts

I like to tell my students to time their putting stroke with a one-two, or "tick-tock," motion. Say to yourself, "tick-tock," as you swing the putter back and through the ball.

The length of your putting stroke should always control the distance you hit the ball. The longer the putt, the longer the stroke. But **no matter the length of the putt, the tempo of the stroke from address to impact should remain constant.**

Thus, on a three-foot putt your stroke would be slower to accommodate the tick-tock; on a 30-foot putt your stroke would be quicker to follow the same two-beat tempo.

A good way to improve your distance control: Use the classic pendulum image of a clock and think "tick-tock" as you stroke the ball.

How to get your stroke to flow

Use these three keys: Longer, slower, lower

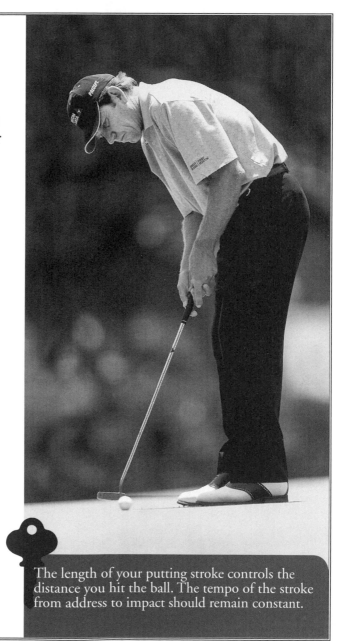

Though Nick Price's fairly abrupt, quick tempo has served him so well with his long game, his aggressive, "rap" type putting stroke has made him a streaky putter at times.

He works hard on the tempo of his stroke—slowing it down, smoothing it out and keeping the putter low to the ground.

Price's focus on his putting "flow" has improved his consistency on the greens. **To get your own putting stroke to flow again, borrow his simple keys: Think longer, slower, lower.**

The length of your putting stroke controls the distance you hit the ball. The tempo of the stroke from address to impact should remain constant.

Give your stroke
a firm foundation
Keep your lower body still

During the putting stroke, your lower body and head need to be as still as the Eiffel Tower. Having **a firm base and rock-steady head enables your shoulders, chest, arms and putter to rock back and then through in unison.** It's this pendulum-style motion that keeps the putterface square through impact, ensuring solid contact with the ball.

Sense a little tension in your knees at address, maintain a solid lower body and say *au revoir* as more putts find the hole.

Stay still over short putts
How to stop 'steering' the ball

The biggest problem among poor putters is excessive body movement, particularly on short putts. **To train your body to remain passive, practice your putting without taking a backswing.**

Push the ball toward the hole using your arms and the shoulders to swing the putterhead. Now incorporate the feeling of your body remaining passive as you take your normal backstroke. Allow the putter to release on the through-stroke without moving your body.

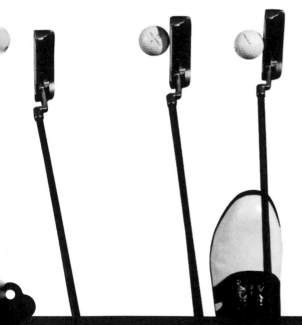

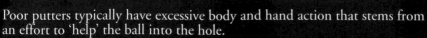

Poor putters typically have excessive body and hand action that stems from an effort to 'help' the ball into the hole.

To make more short putts . . .
Learn to accelerate through the ball

Most players miss short putts because their backstrokes are too long, and **they decelerate through impact.**

Use the tee drill I'm demonstrating here to make more short putts:

• You want to stick a tee in the green about one head-length directly behind the ball.

• Using the tee as a backstop, practice four-foot putts, feeling the shorter motion. (Your real backstroke will be a bit longer.)

• Then accelerate the putterhead through impact to start the ball on your intended line with true roll.

Use this tee drill to ingrain a stroke that's shorter going back and accelerates through the ball. You'll make more short putts.

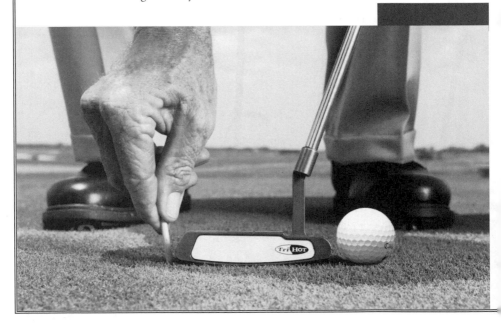

... Practice 'short back, long through'
Control the putter to start the ball on line

It doesn't take much effort to roll a golf ball, but what energy you do need must be controlled. Practicing shortish putts with a tee a few inches behind your putter at address will help you ingrain more of the short, controlled, accelerated "pop" stroke used by good short putters.

On longer putts, however, you need a much lengthier stroke so that you not only accelerate the putterhead but also flow it for good feel.

Remember this simple rule: short putts, short stroke; longer putts, longer stroke. But always accelerate smoothly.

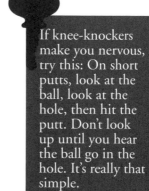

If knee-knockers make you nervous, try this: On short putts, look at the ball, look at the hole, then hit the putt. Don't look up until you hear the ball go in the hole. It's really that simple.

'Palm' your short putts
How to keep the putter on line

To hit more solid and on-line putts, think of your right palm as the putterface. Grip the putter so the pad of the right palm is parallel to the putterface and is aimed toward the target.

Use a shoulder-controlled, pendulum-style motion to swing the putter freely through the ball, with the right palm traveling down the target line. Keep the wrists firm to eliminate any manipulation. **As long as the right palm stays square to the target line, the putterface will, too.**

The right palm (for right-handed golfers) mirrors the putterface. To make more short putts, keep it square to the target line.

126

As the putt gets longer, the putterhead should travel slightly inside the target line on the back and forward swings, then move squarely down the line through impact. It then travels back to the inside on the follow-through. **Attempts to force the putterhead straight back and through on longer putts can result in excessive manipulation of the hands and arms,** which can lead to poor distance control.

To stroke long putts consistently well, imagine you're swinging the putterhead along the rim of a large wheel. With the shoulders, arms and hands moving in unison, allow the putterface to open and close naturally as it follows the arc. Only through impact does the putterface need to be perpendicular to the target line.

On longer putts, trace the rim of a wheel
Allow the putterface to open and close naturally

On short putts, the stroke is straight back, straight through. On long putts, the putter travels along more of an arc.

How to lag long putts close
The 'brush point' is right at the ball

To improve your rhythm on long putts, you want to imagine that you're sweeping the putterblade just as you would sweep a broom. When you brush something with a broom, you don't pick it up steeply and then poke it at the ground; you sweep it. In the same way, **keep the putterblade low to the ground in a wide arc going back and through.**

The brush point—where the bristles would make contact—should be right at the ball. You should have a feeling of release as you follow through.

On a short putt you want to keep the left hand and wrist firm, but on a long putt you need a little bit of flex in the left wrist at the finish. This image, and getting plenty of practice, will help you develop good rhythm and better distance control.

"Sweeping" a long putt helps you get a little body into the motion, which promotes a flowing and rhythmic stroke.

Take the 'hit' out of your stroke

Longer putts require a more flowing motion

Ernie Els is a superb lag putter. He's got great natural tempo and always strokes putts to a flowing, "tick-tock" rhythm, back and through.

During a practice round at the 2004 Sony Open, Ernie saw Michelle Wie using a jabbing-type stroke on long putts. He suggested she lengthen her stroke while keeping the same pace throughout. Michelle's a quick learner; after hearing Ernie's advice she went out a made putts of 60 and 50 feet on Friday, taking just 23 putts for the round.

Keeping a smooth, metronomic rhythm is something we always get back to with Ernie, and all he has to do is be reminded of it if he gets a bit jerky with his own stroke. Now Michelle keeps his tip in mind, and you should too.

After Ernie Els told Michelle Wie to take the "hit" out of her stroke on long putts, she made bombs of 60 and 50 feet.

Swing Flaws:
Fixing Your Faults

Every golfer has swing flaws. ● That's as true for Tiger Woods and Ernie Els and Michelle Wie as it is for you and me. ● It's just that the best golfers find a way to identify their flaws and then fix them as best they can. ● The goal is not to perfect the swing—even Ben Hogan claimed that he only hit one or two "perfect" shots a round. ● My goal in this chapter is to help you become a more confident, consisent golfer by helping you improve the quality of your "misses."

Swing Flaws:
Fixing Your Faults

Trouble-shooting tips to boost
your confidence and consistency

Although we live in a high-tech age with videos and computers used to analyze and dissect swings to the nth degree, **golf, when played well, is still a game based on feelings and simple keys.** Some trial and error is often required to find the right key.

This chapter consists of a selection of drills, feelings and check-points for you to experiment with and to aid your game. Browse through them and try only one at a time. Use them to improve your fundamentals, of course, but keep in mind your ultimate goal: Golf is a game about flow and rhythm, and in having a swing motion that creates the energy needed to hit a golf ball straight and far—time after time.

You never know: With one of these quick tips you could hit the jackpot and make a real difference to your con-sistency and your ability to hit solid shots.

Sergio Garcia chokes down on a long iron when he must find the fairway—or when his driver swing is a little off.

133

Inconsistent off the tee?
Develop a pre-shot routine
Why every golfer needs a waggle

Golfers who start their swing from a stiff, static position—often because of overthinking—are at an immediate disadvantage.

A pre-swing action in golf, whether it's a small movement of the clubhead or a more dynamic "mini-rehearsal" of the takeaway, preps you for the actual swing.

I equate the movement to a basketball player's routine at the foul line. All good free-throw shooters follow a particular routine to get into a set rhythm.

Adopt a similar kind of consistent motion before swinging the club. Experiment and develop a routine that's comfortable for you and easy to repeat. Make it identical on every shot. Not only will it get you settled, it will also allow you to start each swing rhythmically.

PAUL LIPP

Every good free-throw shooter has a consistent pre-shot routine. Follow one yourself to reduce tension and get into a set rhythm.

How to keep your driver in play
Lost your feel mid-round? Simulate impact against a tire

Here's a good on-course drill to help you regain a feel for the clubhead and to boost your clubhead speed through impact: Set up to a golf cart (or ball washer), pressing the clubface into the tire **to feel how the clubhead releases with leverage against the resistance of your body and left arm.**

You'll be amazed at the extra clubhead speed you can generate with this feeling in mind.

Now turn around so the back of your driver presses against the tire. Push back for five seconds, feeling resistance in your right arm. Feel your midsection move and your feet press into the ground. You'll improve how the club sets on the way back and create more leverage as your body turns.

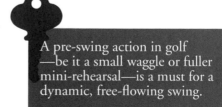

A pre-swing action in golf —be it a small waggle or fuller mini-rehearsal—is a must for a dynamic, free-flowing swing.

Take tension out of your swing
For better balance and rhythm, set up on thin ice

To take the tension out of your legs at address and to promote good balance throughout the swing, imagine you're standing on thin ice. **You want to feel light-footed as you** **prepare to swing, not dug into the ground** like some sumo wrestler girding for battle.

After setting up to the ball, gently waggle your feet as though you're testing the ice to see if it will support you. This thought will help keep you relaxed and ready to begin the motion of your swing from a well-balanced, athletic position.

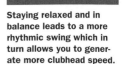

Staying relaxed and in balance leads to a more rhythmic swing which in turn allows you to generate more clubhead speed.

What starts the first move down? It's not your head

How to begin the downswing with the proper sequence of motion

The tendency to slide your head and upper body forward to start the downswing **can lead you to hang back as compensation, resulting in inconsistent contact.** One technique we use to improve Justin Rose's awareness of this error is to accentuate it and then have him work to resist it. As you can see below, I'm pushing Justin's head forward toward the target as he works against me and holds it back. It's a lot more effective than me just telling him, "Don't move your head forward."

The swing is all about feel. Real improvement occurs only when players become aware of their tendencies and the sensations needed to correct them.

To hit straighter shots . . .
Get your feet square first

Most slicers have an alignment problem. Often, it's a chicken-and-egg problem. Their drives fly off to the right so they shift their stance around to the left. This compensation usually leads to a worse slice to the right—or sometimes a solid shot pulled "dead left."

Shots that finish to the right are caused by one thing: an open clubface, or one that is pointing to the right, at impact. Elsewhere in this chapter I'll give you grip, swing and ball-position tips to fix your slice, but here, let's straighten out your body angles.

Proper alignment is essential to hitting the ball more solidly and straighter.

To start straightening out that slice, get square with your feet, then work your way up to your eye line.

... Learn to set up square
Make sure your shoulders are parallel

Many slicers make an effort to set up square by standing so their toe line is parallel to the target line. That's good—but then they open the hips and shoulders to the target.

The shoulders are key; use a club to make sure yours are parallel to the toe line and to the target line. Check yourself in the mirror, or have a friend take a look. Also, lower and relax the right arm at address. Most "banana-ball" slicers have the right arm too high and tense at address. Position your arms at address so that a club held across your foreams is parallel to the target line.

Most slicers have an alignment problem. Learn how to set up square, with your feet, hips, shoulders and eyes all parallel to the target line.

NO

NO

How being off plane wrecks your swing...
Keep the club parallel to the angle of the shaft at address

For the club to accelerate unhindered from the top of the swing through impact, it must travel down on the correct plane. **That plane is parallel to, and slightly above, the angle of the clubshaft as it sat at address.**

A swing plane that's too upright often leads to a weak, out-to-in hit.

A swing plane that's too flat leads to a shallow swing angle of approach that is excessively in to out. This leads to inconsistent contact, and blocks to the right or "flip" hooks to the left.

The goal, of course, is to get in the downswing slot that allows you to return the club regularly, and with power, to its starting point: squarely behind the ball.

A downswing that's more upright *(top)* or more flat *(bottom)* than ideal will force you to make compensations to hit the ball solid.

... And how to find the 'slot'

The key point in the swing to be on plane

YES

Rehearse swinging the club to the top and then to about halfway down, the clubshaft traveling along the proper plane line.

As a guide, stick your golf umbrella or an old clubshaft in the ground parallel to your club at address. Choking down on the grip can help you check the angle on the downswing. Or you can stick a tee in the hole at the butt end of the grip—use it to ensure that **the club-shaft is parallel to and above the umbrella as it swings down.** The club should be right on the umbrella through impact.

The downswing happens so quickly it's tough to consciously control, yet it's the heart of the solid strike. Practice getting into the proper position.

NO

Why your swing flaws may not be all your fault
How poorly fitted clubs can lead to inconsistency

In the photos above I'm using a 5-iron that's at least an inch too short for me and has a fairly flat lie angle. A club that is too short causes your posture at address to become top-heavy. Notice how rounded my back is and how far the club handle is from my belt buckle.

Setting up with your body bent over the ball increases the spine angle. The shoulders turn on an angle that's too tilted, which results in a steep swing plane. **With a poor address posture leading to a poor at-the-top position, a poor downswing and impact will follow.**

Consult your local golf pro to make sure you're playing with properly fitted clubs.

How your clubs are fitted to you will affect your swing. Play irons with the proper length shafts and correct lie angles.

Curing your slice starts with the proper grip

First, hold the club more in the fingers

Moving your left hand to the right, or clockwise on the grip, and placing it more in the fingers, **can help square or even slightly close the clubface at impact and produce a draw.** With this "stronger" grip you should be able to see about 2½ knuckles when you look down at your grip.

You want the right hand placed parallel to your left hand on the club; the line formed between the thumb and the forefinger on each hand must match. The club in this hand should also lie across the fingers, and the lifeline of your right hand needs to be placed on top of the left thumb, as I'm about to do in the photo above. This helps keep the hands working as a unit.

When talking about the grip, "strong" has nothing to do with pressure or tension. It refers to how you position your hands on the grip more toward the right than you would for a "neutral" or "weak" grip.

If your ball flight looks like this . . .

There are two types of slices, and knowing the kind you hit will help you get rid of it. The first type is called **the pull slice.** As you can see here, a pull slice starts left of the target and then curves right—sometimes *way* right (though you hit the occasional pull long and left). The steep, glancing blow of the pull-slicer reduces distance.

Here's what causes you to hit the pull slice and why you get so little distance with that banana ball:

• Your clubhead approaches the ball on a steep angle relative to the correct plane (an out-to-in path);

• The clubface is open at impact;

• The clubhead decelerates before impact;

• The arms collapse through impact;

• You have a short, off-balance follow-through.

Opposite are two ways to straighten out the pull slice.

The pull slice occurs when the club approaches the ball on an outside-to-in swing path with the club-face open at impact.

. . . Do this

Most pull-slicers have a "weak" grip—the hands are placed around to the left of the handle. **Adopt a stronger grip.** Move both hands around to the right so they are parallel to each other, as I'm demonstrating at right.

. . . And this

Most pull-slicers play the ball too far forward. **Moving the ball slightly back in the stance encourages the pull-slicer to swing more from the inside, on a shallower plane.** Play the ball a couple of inches inside your left heel, as I'm showing at right.

You're a pull-slicer if you:
• Aim left to allow for your curving ball flight.
• Hit the occasional pop-up with your driver.
• Often miss short and right with your irons.

If your ball flight looks like this . . .

Many push-slicers have a fairly athletic swing, with the power and speed to hit the ball far. The problem is that those wild shots can go way right, as I'm demonstrating in the photo at right.

Read on for a list of what typically causes you to hit **the push slice:**
• The clubhead swings down too much from inside the target line;
• The clubface is open at impact;
• Your hips are too active on the downswing, with the arms lagging behind;
• There's a loss of posture at impact (you lose the spine angle established at address);
• Your hands have to be too active to compensate for the open clubface;
• The rhythm, or sequencing, of your swing is poor.

On the next page are tips to help you fix the push slice—and get rid of those blowup holes that prevent you from shooting good scores.

The push slice starts right, then curves farther right—the result of an open clubface and in-to-out swing path.

Do this . . .

Most push-slicers have the club too much in the left-hand palm. Check your left-hand grip. **Place the club more down in the fingers.**

You're a push-slicer if you:
• Dread O.B. right.
• Top or thin your irons.
• Hit shots off the toe.
• Hit an occasional duck hook.
• Have trouble from rough.

And this . . .

Playing the ball a little farther forward than standard can help the push-slicer square up the clubface at impact. For the driver, **position the ball in line with your left heel,** as I'm doing at right.

How to turn an "over-the-top" slice . . .
Groove a flatter downswing plane

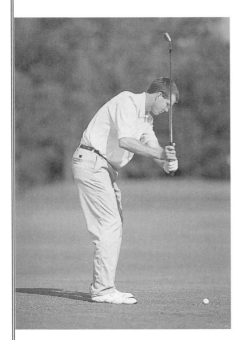

As this slicer is demonstrating, coming "over the top" with the arms and upper body on the downswing brings the clubshaft into a nearly vertical position. The hands will pull the club weakly back toward the body, resulting in the arms collapsing through impact, and a loss of power and direction.

Ideally, you want to swing the club down on a plane that is parallel to the position it was in at address. **Players who hit from the top swing the club far above and outside the ideal swing plane.** The clubhead coming down gets too much in front of the body and results in an outside-in swing path. If the clubface is square through impact, the shot will fly to the left; if it's open—as is likely—it will start left, then curve way right.

The key to solving this problem is in getting the clubhead more behind the player on the downswing.

A downswing that's too steep can cause you to lose power and direction.

. . . Into an inside-out draw swing
Shallow out your approach

Practice hitting balls from a lie several inches above your feet. Use a middle iron and choke down on the club slightly. This drill is effective in developing **a more rounded swing in which the arms and hands can release the club more from the inside.** Think "baseball swing" instead of "chopping wood."

Hitting balls above your feet promotes a shallower angle of approach, which allows the club to return to the ball on a plane matching the one established at address, resulting in a more inside-out swing path. With a clubface that's square to closing through impact, you make a powerful draw, instead of a weak slice.

Coming over the top with the arms and upper body results in a weak, high slice. Learn to swing the club more *around* your body.

To prevent an early turn . . .

Don't drag the club too inside on the backswing

Having your hands too far behind the body can lead to an excessive in-to-out or out-to-in swing path.

A common sight among players with swing-path problems is that halfway back the hands are too far behind the body. For better players who start the downswing with their hips, this can lead to a path that's too in-to-out. For poorer players who tend to start the downswing with their upper bodies, this can lead to an exaggerated out-to-in swing path.

Initiate the swing with a push away from the target with the left arm and shoulder. This helps prevent the right side of the body from turning away too quickly and dragging the arms and club inside with it.

... Keep your hands in front of your chest
Initiate the swing with the left arm and shoulder

To feel the correct position of the hands as you swing the club back, try the left-arm-only drill. Grip your left wrist with your right hand and guide the left arm and club to the proper position halfway back.

As the left shoulder is pushed away smoothly from the target, the hands should remain in front of the chest. The goal is to have the left arm positioned slightly across the chest, so the club can then swing up over the right shoulder, rather than behind it.

The farther inside the clubhead gets on the backswing, the more compensations you have to make on the downswing.

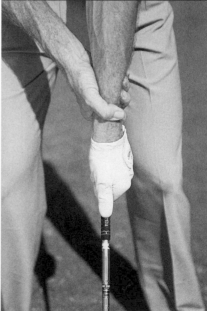

To make solid contact . . .
Square the face with the split-hands drill

The split-hands drill helps you feel the rotation of the forearms as your body turns and your arms swing through impact.

The key to consistency is to find the right blend of body, hand and arm action.

In the modern athletic swing, an "active," rotating body through impact plays a big role in releasing the clubhead, with the hands and forearms being fairly passive. There is no need to have the right hand and forearm aggressively cross over the left, as a rapidly closing clubface through impact can result in big hooks.

However, **there are many golfers—seniors and slicers, especially—who would benefit from this type of "cross-over" release.** On the next page I'll show you how the split-hands drill can help both the hooker and the slicer time the release of the forearms better, with square contact the result.

...Find the right blend of arm, body action
Fight hooks and slices by learning the proper release

This drill, where you separate your hands about an inch and use a 7-iron off the tee, can benefit everybody.

To fight a slice or add power: Use the split-hands drill to encourage the right hand and forearm to cross over the left. As I'm demonstrating in the photo at right, the goal is to sense the chest being more square through impact—it's facing more toward the ball—with the right hand and forearm on top of the left.

To fight a hook: Better players, who typically struggle with overactive hands and arms, can use the split-hands drill to promote a better turn of the chest and torso through the ball. This will allow you to maintain a square clubface at impact. Here the image would be one of the chest being open at impact—it's facing more toward the target—with the right hand and forearm more under the left.

Ideally, as it approaches the ball, the clubface should be squaring slowly in tandem with the rotating torso.

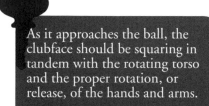

As it approaches the ball, the clubface should be squaring in tandem with the rotating torso and the proper rotation, or release, of the hands and arms.

How to avoid 'getting stuck'
Slow the lower body to allow the arms to catch up

Like a lot of athletic young swingers, Charles Howell has such a quick lower-body movement that his arm swing sometimes trails coming through the hitting zone. Below I'm using a stretch band to help him **create a feeling of resistance in the legs.** The rubber band slows the lower body and encourages a more active arm swing.

Here's a drill you can perform by yourself if you tend to hit blocks and hooks: Hit balls with a closed stance. Align the toe of your right foot with the arch of your left foot. This will prevent your lower body from clearing too quickly.

Here Charles Howell works on slowing his lower-body movement to better time his arm swing and body turn through the ball.

Tired of blocked shots to the right?

Use the feet-together drill to feel a freer release

For many amateurs who allow the lower body to outpace the hands and arms to impact, the result is this: The clubface never squares up. Instead it remains open as it pushes the ball off to the right.

To help stabilize the lower body through impact, with a freer release of the arms, hit balls with your feet about nine inches apart. It forces you to turn more through the shot with the arms and body in sync. Feel your arms moving through, the right forearm rotating over the left, as your upper body turns through the shot. This more in-sync motion allows you to square the clubface naturally, without having to manipulate it with your hands as they try to play catch-up with the body.

Some players have overactive lower bodies; some rely too much on the arms and upper body. The key is the proper blend of both.

To prevent a reverse pivot . . .

Don't think 'keep your eye on the ball'

Golfers who are overly concerned with keeping their eye on the ball and the head down restrict their body turn and limit, or even reverse, the weight shift. Often this is caused by relying too much on a dominant right eye. **Right-eye dominant golfers need to learn to use the left eye to look at the ball during the backswing.** The rotation of your head facilitates the rotation of your shoulders and upper body behind the ball.

NO

Keeping your right eye focused on the ball can result in a poor weight shift and loss of power.

YES

... Learn how to shift your weight fully
Allow your head to shift laterally

If you have a problem with a reverse pivot or getting behind the ball, practice hitting balls with your right eye closed. (At my schools we use an eye patch.) **Focus on allowing your head to move as the body turns.**

To swing with power, especially with the driver, you have to get behind the ball, shifting your weight to your right side as you swing back. It may be a bit difficult at first, but the result will be longer tee shots.

As the body rotates during the backswing, the head moves a little laterally and should rotate slightly as well.

How to keep from sliding through impact
Practice in bare feet to improve balance and stability

Practicing in bare feet can help you achieve the stable balance in the swing that is common to all good golfers.

On the backswing, feel your weight shift onto the inside of your right foot. On the fol-low-through, **feel the weight on the inside of your left foot, rather than allowing it to roll over.** This will reduce the tendency to slide the lower body through impact, and it will help you rotate the hips as you should. A finish that has you "on your toes" with the right heel point-ing straight up will guarantee a complete weight shift.

On the finish, keep your left foot flat on the ground and fully supporting your weight to promote a full release of the right side.

Improve your impact position
Put the brakes on your left side

Your legs provide the resistance against which you wind and unwind your trunk. Through impact, **the left side of your body must be firm enough to both support and promote the release of the clubhead as your upper body unwinds.**

At impact, feel as though your left leg is bracing or straightening. "Putting the brakes" on your left side prevents the lower body from sliding through impact.

It enables the upper body to unwind fully for maximum power. The arms and hands then accelerate through the ball at the proper time, which helps square up the clubface for consistent contact.

PAUL LIPP

Though there's truth to the adage "drive your legs for power," many golfers overuse their legs. A firmer left leg can mean more power.

Seeking stability?
Give yourself a lesson in the sand

A good exercise to help calm your body action is to set yourself in a fairway bunker and practice hitting iron shots without digging your feet into the sand.

I give this drill to better golfers, especially young players, whose lower-body action tends to outrace the arms.

As you set up, be aware of your feet, and be sensitive to the balance your lower body must provide to get the club back down in front of you. Players who have a violent downswing and slide or clear their hips too early can sometimes get away with it on a firm surface, but **with the weak foundation of the sand, any dramatic change in the center of gravity is magnified.**

Use a middle iron, stand on top of the sand and focus on hitting solid shots without excessive movement of the lower body.

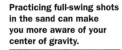

Practicing full-swing shots in the sand can make you more aware of your center of gravity.

Support from the ground up is important if you want to strike the ball solidly. Stability comes with controlled movement of the lower body.

For more clubhead speed . . .

Improve your wrist action and increase your leverage

Poor wrist action is a major reason for inconsistency and lack of distance. The ability to cock your wrists on the backswing and then hold that cocked position well into the downswing is what is needed to strike the ball solidly.

For some golfers, a conventional grip can place excessive pressure on the club in the middle of the grip, **making it difficult to freely cock and uncock the wrists.**

Experiment with these two "double" grips; start with the short irons, and see how it goes.

The double interlock (*left*) adds leverage to the grip; the double overlap (*right*) makes the hands feel very compact on the grip.

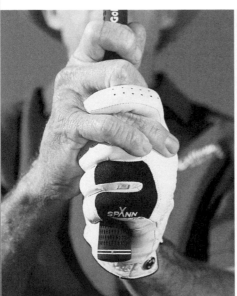

... Try 'doubling up' on your grip
Create more lag on the downswing

In experimenting, I have found that by taking the grip (overlapping or interlocking) with two fingers as opposed to one, the pressure in the middle of the grip is lessened. It's then easier to increase grip pressure in the last three fingers of the left hand and also the index finger and thumb of the right hand. Because less of your right hand is on the club, **a double grip makes it easier to set the club on the backswing and hold the lag on the downswing.**

Jim Furyk uses a double overlap grip; you might want to try doubling up as well. Give it a try if you are having trouble with your wrist cock—it may give you more snap at impact and therefore more power.

Having too much tension in your hands inhibits the natural cocking of the wrists, resulting in an early release and a weak hit.

What to do when your ball's in a divot
Just remove the 'yolk'

When they find it lying in a divot hole, most golfers try to "lift" the ball out with a scooping motion. The likely result is a fat shot—and even more frustration.

To make solid contact, imagine the ball is an egg yolk, the divot hole the egg white. You want to hit only the yolk. **Move the ball back in your stance and position your hands and weight more forward.** Keep your hands ahead of the ball through impact. Allow for the ball to fly low and run far.

To hit the ball cleanly from a divot hole, set up to create a sharper, more descending angle into the ball.

In trouble? Assess the risk and don't get greedy
How to handle trouble like a chess master

Bernhard Langer's ability to plot his way around a golf course, like a chess grandmaster working out his strategy, is uncanny. Below you see Langer extricating himself from knee-high rough. You can bet that before he played this shot, he had picked a spot that he wanted to hit his next shot from, and that he had **taken into account the risk factors and was not going to get greedy.**

The lesson for amateurs is to make sure you get yourself out of trouble and back in play at all costs. Play the percentage shot. Don't hope to hit a miracle shot, which could be even more costly.

We all hit into trouble at times. The key is to minimize the error. Hit the percentage shot, even if it's just a sand wedge to get back into play.

How to hit great under pressure
'Replay' your best shot ever

I once played in an 18-hole scramble with a high-handicapper who was having a miserable day. Standing on the tee of the final hole, he knew that our foursome needed to use his tee shot.

I told him to think back to the time when he had hit his best tee shot ever. "Remember exactly how you felt at that moment," I said "and **keep that thought process in mind as you take your practice swing and set up to the ball.**"

He said he would.

You guessed it: He absolutely nailed it.

Replay an old "tape" from your memory bank, calling up a success rather than dwelling on a negative thought.

Think 'target,' not 'golf swing'

Keep your swing thoughts simple

Too many players stand over the ball with intense mechanical swing thoughts that just create tension.

Focus on the target, and use **one simple pre-swing key that helps you generate good mechanics without overthinking.** It's a form of positive thinking that translates mechanics into feel, reducing tension and allowing you to focus on your primary objective: getting the ball to go where you want it to go.

The pros realize that getting too mechanical can hurt their performance. Stick to one simple swing key.

AFTERWORD

I hope you've enjoyed reading these quick tips from David Leadbetter as much as I've liked working on my game with him. Whether it's at a tour event, on the practice range of his academy in Florida or over the Internet e-mailing videos from my home in Hawaii, it's been a great experience for me. He looks at my swing and then shows me a new drill or feel to try, and I'm like, "OK—I can do that." And 20 minutes later I'm back on track.

I can honestly say that not once have I not hit the ball better when I've tried a new drill that David's suggested. In the past year we've shortened my backswing a little and tried to get everything more synchronized going back. With a slower, more rhythmic backswing, I can actually get more speed coming down. My swing is more reliable now than it's ever been—and I know there are still quite a few more yards to find off the tee. My short game is so much better, too.

I'm ready to take on any new challenges. Are you? Then let me give you *my* challenge: Put David's quick tips to work for you. I know you'll be rewarded with a more reliable swing, lower scores and more fun out on the golf course.

Well, what are you waiting for?

Michelle Wie
Honolulu
February 2006

ABOUT THE AUTHORS

In addition to his monthly columns and regular instruction features in Golf Digest, David Leadbetter has written six golf instruction books and many best-selling videotapes and DVDs. Originally from Worthing in Sussex, England, Leadbetter began his career in golf on the European and South African Tours. Soon after he retired from playing, he began to incorporate his teaching methods and philosophies into a stringent training program, which has led to the establishment of 27 David Leadbetter Golf Academies worldwide. He's the personal swing coach for numerous tour professionals, including Nick Price, Ernie Els and Michelle Wie. To find out more about his golf schools, books and teaching aids, visit www.davidleadbetter.com.

Scott Smith (*left*) has been writing instruction articles with David Leadbetter since 1996. He's now the editor of GolfDigest.com, which features the complete archive of Leadbetter articles and interviews. Find it at www.golfdigest.com/leadbetter.